WHITE MONEY/BLACK POWER

WHITE MONEY/ BLACK POWER

The Surprising History of African American Studies
and the Crisis of Race in Higher Education

Noliwe M. Rooks

BEACON PRESS, BOSTON

Beacon Press
25 Beacon Street
Boston, Massachusetts 02108-2892
www.beacon.org

Beacon Press books
are published under the auspices of
the Unitarian Universalist Association of Congregations.

10 09 08 07   8 7 6 5 4 3 2 1

This book is printed on acid-free paper that meets the uncoated paper
ANSI/NISO specifications for permanence as revised in 1992.

Text design by Patricia Duque Campos
Composition by Wilsted & Taylor Publishing Services

Library of Congress Cataloging-in-Publication Data

Rooks, Noliwe M.
  White money/Black power : the surprising history of African American
studies and the crisis of race in higher education / Noliwe M. Rooks.
    p. cm.
  Includes bibliographical references and index.
  ISBN-13: 978-0-8070-3271-8 (pbk. : alk. paper) 1. African Americans—
Study and teaching (Higher)—History—20th century. 2. Education, Higher—
Economic aspects—United States—History—20th century. 3. African
Americans—Education (Higher)—History—20th century. 4. Ford
Foundation—History—20th century. 5. United States—Race relations—
History—20th century. 6. Black power—United States—History—
20th century. 7. African American college students—History—20th century.
8. Student movements—United States—History—20th century. I. Title.

E184.7.R66 2005
973'.0496073'00711—dc22
2005014708

For my son, Jelani, who has
waited almost patiently for me
to dedicate a book to him.
It's my pleasure to do so now.

CONTENTS

WHITE MONEY/BLACK POWER

The Ford Foundation and Black Studies

In 1968, while under the leadership of McGeorge Bundy, the former national security advisor in both the Kennedy and Johnson administrations, the Ford Foundation began to craft and then fund a strategy aimed at ensuring a complication-free birth and life for African American Studies on college campuses. It was an act that would be denounced by the United States Congress as an attempt at social engineering. In keeping with the late-1960s world-view, African American Studies (then termed Black Studies) was envisioned and proposed by the Ford Foundation as a means to desegregate and integrate the student bodies, faculties, and curricula of colleges and universities in ways that would mirror the public school systems that had been ordered by the Supreme Court to free themselves from "separate but equal" racial educational systems. Within that context, African American Studies programs were viewed as a positive response to the increasingly strident calls for social and political redress made by African American students, as well as a means of responding to the unprecedented increase in the numbers of African American students entering colleges and universities during that politically turbulent period.

Those early strategies around institutionalizing Black Studies, funded by Bundy and the Ford Foundation, currently threaten the very viability of African American Studies and have implications for how we think about, discuss, and understand both affirmative action and racial integration within colleges and universities today. While African American Studies programs and departments are still a central means of ensuring broad-based discussions about race, as well as the presence of Black students and faculty in American higher education, there has been a truly ironic development: As "Black Studies" became "African American, Africana, and African Diaspora Studies," Black students and faculty on white college campuses were less frequently African American—a trend that has increased. Indeed, the very question of what we mean when we say "Black students" has become a contested issue in and of itself. In 2005, increasing numbers of Black students are the children or grandchildren of first- or second-generation immigrants from the Caribbean or Africa. These students compose between 40 to nearly 80 percent of Black students on elite college campuses. In short, Black no longer means African American. As a result, if Black Studies was originally a tool used by colleges and universities to foster integration of faculties and curricula, and to achieve social justice, by recruiting African American students and faculty, today such programs have begun to signal a compelling shift in what we mean when we speak of affirmative action in relation to Black students. This is a far cry from the circumstances surrounding Black Studies at its founding, and a very different set of concerns from those McGeorge Bundy and the Ford Foundation first sought to address.

Much of this book is about student protest, the politics of racial integration on college campuses, and the politics surrounding the creation of the first departments of African American Studies. The story centers on a history of student protest traditions that are raced in ways not always acknowledged, and covers a time when violence and militancy, wrapped in the rhetoric of Black nationalism, were embraced as a viable strategy to effect social change. It is this latter point that is generally the most difficult to appreciate as we gaze back at a time not far removed from the present. While it was difficult for many in 1968 to accept the rhetoric around the political and social changes called for by students—a rhetoric that demanded colleges and universities discard their antiquated ideas about what constituted an educated individual—no one anticipated the institutional changes or the violence that would erupt when student protest began to center on a desire for a "relevant" education, an education that was capable both of helping to radicalize students and of addressing and ending the racial and economic inequities in the United States. On hundreds of campuses, students linked such calls for relevancy to the formation of Black Studies programs and departments. In halls hallowed and profane, with walls ivied or unadorned, in locales northern, southern, eastern and western, the arrival of Black Studies on predominantly white college campuses was often announced and preceded by cries of "Black Power!" and clenched fists raised in what was universally understood to be the Black Power salute. There were usually calls for increased levels of financial aid for Black students, and demands for the hiring of Black faculty who would teach a radical new curriculum that would educate, empower, and ultimately free not just the students taking the classes, but all Black people. At times the raised hands held signs; on other occasions, they clutched rifles or guns. Sometimes the hands were empty and raised only to cover heads as violent blows rained down.

Two things stand out from that period that are particularly relevant to the student strike that led to the founding of the first department of Black Studies. First, during the period, students offered a profound critique of the society's handling of racial exclusion, and second, the broad participation of white and brown college students in demands for an end to elitist and Eurocentric higher education was widespread. This second point is not widely known. Indeed, when I was writing this book, and told people it was about the history and contemporary meaning

of Black Studies, the response, given the association between the
field and Black student unrest, was generally something like:
"That should be really exciting. It's about time someone focused
on what Black students were up to back then." I rarely told people that what fascinated me was not necessarily the protest of
Black students, but the fact that the first student strike—leading
to the first department of Black Studies—was decidedly interracial and democratic. Those who participated sought nothing
less than a fundamental reorganization of the aims of higher
education.

This is one of the unremarked-upon legacies of the movement that spawned Black Studies as a field in America. Although
the familiar narrative chronicling the beginning of Black Studies
generally centers on Black student protest and violence, in reality, at San Francisco State, Black, white, Native American,
Asian, and Latino students rose up together, joined forces, and
made or supported unequivocal demands. Eighty percent of
the 18,000 students supported the strike by refusing to attend
classes. Thousands of students and faculty staffed daily picket
lines, holding signs declaring, "This Strike Is Against Racism."
Many politicians in California believed that the strike was a sign
that communism or anarchy was poised to rule the day, and just
as many students believed that a cultural and social revolution
was under way. Within that context, a department of Black
Studies was both fought for and feared. Its existence meant very
different things to many different constituencies. The battle
waged on many college campuses sought to realign and redefine
the very meaning of democracy, citizenship, and social justice. If
America was to live up to the ideals of inclusion so much at the
heart of the civil rights movement and the historic *Brown v.
Board of Education* decision, college campuses would need to
provide an accessible education. Education would have to be
inviting to poor and disenfranchised students of all races, but especially to nonwhite students.

I rarely went into such detail when giving the two-sentence description of the book. Crafting a narrative about the beginning of Black Studies that includes white, Asian, Latino, and Native American students is so far removed from what most people think of when conjuring the history of the field, that it necessitates a fundamental rethinking of what many believe to be self-evident facts. Overwhelmingly, history has forgotten that any but Black students were ever involved in the student strike that produced Black Studies at San Francisco State. Perhaps, then, it is not surprising that attempts to reinsert white students into that history can sound a discordant note and disrupt comforting visual, historical, and oral narratives. Certainly, when my thirteen-year-old son watches newsreel footage of the police attacking striking students at San Francisco State, he does not take particular note of the images of police officers pointing guns at, pushing, beating, and arresting Black student protesters. He does, however, notice and comment on each and every white student who is bloodied by batons wielded by the white police officers. "But those are WHITE people they are beating," he repeats with a mantralike regularity. Because he has grown up surrounded by discussions and images of Black protest in many different eras, I did not initially understand what was causing his comments. I came to realize that his response had as much to do with his familiarity with civil rights–era images of African Americans under assault by a Southern police force, as it did with his unfamiliarity with images of whites suffering similar kinds of brutal attacks. It became clear after his first ten minutes of viewing the footage that he had certainly not envisioned that a movement centering on Black freedom could have been interracial. He did not know that any but African Americans could have had an interest and investment in racial and social justice. Images of firehoses shooting water, dogs attacking, and batons raining down on the heads of those who look so much like my son are ubiquitous, raised to the level of art by the photographers who chronicled the movement to end legal segregation in the South. As a result, he sees, but in many ways does not notice, the Black bodies sacrificed at the altar of democracy and equality in those same photographs. Such images are for him historical relics from another era; as he once said, when he was about five, "Martin Luther King freed the slaves in the south." However, he has rarely if ever seen cries of "Black Power" accompanied by scenes of police brutality against whites. He had certainly never heard the story narrated by a white singer intoning the words to a hastily written song, as he accompanied himself on the guitar: "Brother Malcolm went to Mecca, to see what he could see. He saw that we all must be brothers and we must fight for liberty. And we must fight for what is right. Niggers of the world unite. For whites to get behind now is right." Such an image would probably bring many of us up short.[1]

"Did they know they were protesting for Black Studies?" my son asks me and his father and the television and himself. They did know, but the story, given the complicated nature of the period, is much more complex than he can ever imagine.

Racial inclusion, white philanthropy, and historical memory are ultimately at the center of the creation story of African American Studies and at the core of this book. In many ways, the question of memory is the most difficult to do justice to here, and that question once led me to wonder if this was a story I should indeed share.

A STORY TO PASS ON

There are no monuments, holidays, or commemorative stamps that ask us as a nation to mark the founding moment for Black Studies programs. It is difficult even to determine the moment that led to the founding of the first department. Was it at San Francisco State College, where the first department was ulti mately started in 1969, as a result of an ugly and protracted student strike, or was the Black student strike at Howard University in March of 1968 the most significant event? Howard's was the first of many student strikes to come, and it set the tone and strategy for increasingly radicalized and militant students in all parts of the United States, including those at San Francisco State. It is telling that we as a country do not grapple with or debate questions such as these concerning the founding of Black Studies.

In fact, the late 1960s and early 1970s are largely absent from our discussions of political promise and multiracial dreams. There are no heartrending calls on the part of leaders, elected or not, to reflect upon the sacrifice of those who died or were injured in an effort to institute Black Studies departments. There is little in our shared culture that reminds us that the Black Power movement happened and that one of its lasting contributions was the formation of Black Studies departments and programs. If we reflect on it at all, we tend to remember the period as a jumble of images: cities burning, Black fists raised in a salute, and Afros framing Black faces. Nonetheless, *how* we remember matters.

Memory is both public and private, both historical and contemporary. Increasingly, as I attempt to make sense of the key moments, upheavals, court rulings, personalities, and historical context of the period when Black Studies was first instituted, and grapple with the question of what such programs and departments mean today, I wonder if how we remember tells us more about our past or our present. Is the movement that birthed Black Studies programs and departments a historical relic, a cultural occasion for self-congratulatory glad-handing, or the foundation of programs that today function as a path towards a collectively envisioned future? The period explored in this book, from 1968 to 2005, captured America's cultural imagination and complicated the nature of our collective conversations about race. As a result, both the period of time and the subject matter raise questions about legacy, which is to say, the ways in which we commemorate and remember who we are as a country and what our present says about our future. Thinking about, remembering, contextualizing, and understanding the past and present of Black Studies programs matters. It matters not only because such programs tell us so much about whence we have come and the progress we have made, but also because the field will be central for us as a way to make sense of our country's increasingly complicated present and future in regard to race.

Black Studies programs, departments, and institutes have had a long, contentious, yet revealing, relationship with America's institutions of higher education and have played a compelling role within the imaginings of this nation's popular consciousness. The creation and institutionalization of Black Studies is sometimes viewed as a result of the capitulation of well-meaning white college administrators to militant, angry, and ungrateful African American students who were recruited to Northern colleges and universities during the late 1960s. The role of Black Studies in such universities is often thought of, at best, as utilitarian, as a means to ensure a comfortable social space for the institution's Black students, or, at worst, as glorified affirmative action programs useful for ensuring an easy ride for unqualified Black students. However, Black Studies is rarely viewed as a successful example of social justice, a means of multiracial democratic reform, or a harbinger of widespread institutional and cultural change in relation to race, integration, and desegregation at the postsecondary level. That is precisely what these programs were, and what they tell us today about the role and meaning of race in higher education, about the battle for "African Americans to be a full and accepted part of the scholarly enterprise" is no less instructive than it was thirty years ago, when the first programs and departments were established.[7]

In the past, the primary concerns about Black Studies involved ways to legitimize the new field.[3] In 2005, the issues are far more wide-ranging. Whether we like to acknowledge the fact or not, race is a central feature of American culture and society. However, we as a culture are not well practiced in taking the complexity of race into account and having mature societal conversations about its significance, institutionally, historically, or personally. To the extent that we talk about racial difference at all, we prefer to speak about "diversity," or bring up race merely to dismiss its importance. Black Studies offers us all a way of theorizing about race and racial difference that is more important now than ever before. The story of Black Studies' relationship to our contemporary period is central, little known, and important, and it concerns how and why we remember as we do.

REMEMBERING FREEDOM

In the final pages of *Beloved,* by Nobel laureate Toni Morrison, the characters come to believe that the novel's narrative of racial trauma, historical violence, and cultural memory "is not a story to pass on." Understanding that this history has real power in the present and that memories both harm and heal, they choose to forget, as an act of self-protection. I too have continued to ask myself, while writing *White Money/Black Power,* "Is it a story to pass on?" Could it be that this narrative is best left undisturbed? Given my belief that there is an important story to be told about the thicket of relationships among white philanthropy, America's changing struggles with racial integration at the university level, and the field of African American Studies, I have answered the question in the affirmative. Yet I do so understanding that clarity does not always ameliorate the significance of memory, and that intent cannot control the use of memory in the service of power.

The stories, incidents, and history discussed here as a part of the founding of African American Studies mattered profoundly to those involved, and they evoke powerfully remembered emotions from a time before African Americans could assume their acceptance in America's colleges and universities. Little has been written about the formation of such programs, and less still about what they mean in relation to contemporary racial politics in higher education. That scarcity makes the story told here matter all the more. Although no wounds discussed here are as raw as those explored in Morrison's novel of antebellum filicide, the result nonetheless touches exposed nerves never allowed the space, time, and treatment to heal. Such is often the case when the topic is race, racism, inclusion, and the ownership of history in America.

Accordingly, as I talked to people about wanting to write a book about the history, meaning, and significance of African American Studies as a field—and in relation to changing and often chaotic racial and cultural dynamics within America in general and the academy in particular—it became clear that for some the very suggestion that the field could have been substantially influenced by the aims, goals, and actions of a white philanthropic organization was less than comforting. For them, people who had fought and sometimes suffered bodily injury and/or material loss for the cause, the formation of hundreds of African American Studies programs on college campuses in the late 1960s and early 1970s meant more than a mere opportunity to engage in study about the history and literature of people of African descent; it represented a hard-won success story from the civil rights/Black Power era. Within that narrative, African American students were the main characters and solely responsible for asking for and receiving racial acknowledgment, acceptance, and most importantly, resources and respect. Black people had risen up, stood tall, and demanded what was right; that standing and the success of their rising had nothing to do with white philanthropy. The resulting programs are a lasting reminder of a moment of self-determination and collective action of a sort rarely experienced by living generations of African Americans. They represent power. What, they asked, could possibly be gained by exploring a relationship between the development of the field and a white philanthropic organization? Victories are important, successes matter, and I began to think that perhaps historical memory should not be tampered with if the impact is to lessen either.

Others I spoke with were concerned that *White Money/Black Power* would look too closely at African American Studies, with the unintended consequence of weakening an already tenuous hold on resources and institutional respect for this relatively nascent discipline. By way of context, remember that in 2002, Harvard president Larry Summers made front-page news when he objected to Professor Cornel West's spoken word CD, activism on behalf of Al Sharpton, and lack of sufficient scholarship that he deemed "appropriate" and befitting a Harvard faculty member. In response to Summers's views becoming public information, House Majority Leader Dick Armey, never too shy to speak his mind, called African American programs "pure junk" and labeled them all "Crib courses."[4] Other commentators chimed in, suggesting that African American college students were simply using the discipline to take the easy road through college. These opinions held sway despite the fact that few African American students actually major in the field even when it is available, which is only in 27 percent of colleges and universities. Indeed, African American students attending one of the other 73 percent of the nation's institutions of higher education have no opportunity to major in the field, even if they want to. Moreover, there are few African American Studies programs at the nation's historically Black colleges and universities, and those schools continue to grant about one-quarter of all bachelor's degrees earned by African Americans.[5]

Selected Sample of Enrolled Black Students
Who Are Majoring in Black Studies—2003[6]

Duke	11.8
Dartmouth	8.6
Brown	8.0
Columbia	5.7
Stanford	2.8
Harvard	2.8
Berkeley	2.0
U-Virginia	1.7
Cornell	1.0
Emory	1.0
U-Chicago	1.0
Yale	1.0
U-Michigan	0.7

In the present political climate—in which claiming and proclaiming racial affiliation and distinction too loudly may brand one as un-American, needlessly divisive, and in search of a heaping handout of affirmative action—there was naturally concern that too much attention to the history of Black Studies would bring more damaging publicity. As Cornel West has opined, "An oppressed people are a paranoid people. But that doesn't mean they're crazy." However, from a third group, I repeatedly heard that a narrative about the beginning of the field was sorely needed. One person admitted that a book focusing on the increase in numbers of Black students and the simultaneous decline in both the size of the African American population on college campuses and the role of African American Studies departments would "confirm my sanity." That alone convinces me that it is a book worth writing and a story worth telling.

White Money/Black Power is organized in two main parts. The first is historical, and the second focuses on the legacy and relationship of the earlier period to today. In the first section, educational change and institutional validation asked for at gunpoint, or with a threat of violence, is but one theme. Indeed, that story is told within the context of the changes that were afoot as a result of widespread changes in the culture of American colleges and universities in general. Within that context, ideas about what education was supposed to be, and for whom it should be geared, loomed large.

RACE, HIGHER EDUCATION, AND THE AMERICAN UNIVERSITY

Although the great majority of *White Money/Black Power* covers the period between 1967 and 2005, and discusses the growth in university population propelled by increased numbers of Black students, it is important in this context to note that in the 1940s, the trend toward growth in the university was propelled by the arrival of G.I.s following World War II. They were a massive population of diverse social classes who, before the enactment of the GI Bill, would only have been able to obtain a college education through night schools or city colleges.[7] Although expansion of colleges and universities in the late 1960s was fueled by new forms of financial aid for students with modest incomes, the GI Bill allowed returning veterans to have most, if not all, of their college tuition paid by the federal government. Within the first few years of its passage, the reality of a college education was within reach of hundreds of thousands of people not previously able to afford it, and the overall number of university and college students more than doubled in the decade between 1955 and 1965. To put what that means into perspective, the figure of over three million additional students during the decade approximated the total number of college students during the preceding three centuries.[8] This included an unprecedented growth in the number of African American students.

Before 1950, given the realities of racial segregation in the

South, if African Americans were to be educated in a white college or university, they would probably have to travel North. Accordingly "the overall enrollment of African Americans outside of the south was somewhere around 61,000 which represented about 47% of African American college students but was a little less than 3% of the total college enrollment."[9] Thus, almost half of African Americans seeking a post-secondary education did so in white Northern institutions, but the overall numbers were still negligible in relation to the total enrollment of Americans in college. However, between 1967, one year before the first department of Black Studies was instituted, and 1977, during the height of the creation of such programs, Black enrollment in colleges and universities increased dramatically. By 1971 African American students represented 8.4 percent of total college enrollment and by 1977, African Americans represented over 10 percent of all college students in the United States. These increases resulted from aggressive recruitment on the part of Northern institutions and large increases in financial aid available from the federal government.[10]

In the 1950s some support for African American students was available through the National Scholarship Service and the Fund for Negro Students, which were later augmented by the National Defense Student Loan Program in 1958 and the National Achievement Program in 1964. However, the growth of African American enrollment in 1967 was preceded by the Higher Education Act of 1965, which provided funds for education through the Work Study Program, Education Opportunity Grants, and the Guaranteed Student Loan Program. These programs were further aided by the creation in 1972 of the Basic Educational Opportunity Grant Program, which granted funds that students were allowed to use to attend the institution of their choice.[11]

The expressed purpose of these types of financial aid programs was to make it possible for more African American students to attend white, Northern institutions. College officials hoped that the presence of more African American students on their campuses would help them to eradicate the vestiges of racism. College officials also believed that the students they recruited would feel gratitude for the collegiate opportunity. Additionally, in their fervor to participate in the legal changes called for by the *Brown v. Board of Education* decision of 1954, which called for an end to segregated school systems and decreed that integration should take place "with all deliberate speed," many Northern institutions lowered standards for admission and established remedial programs specifically aimed at increasing the numbers of African American students they could attract, retain, and educate.

Gratitude was only one of the emotions many of these students felt, and those feelings were often overrun by resentment toward the overwhelmingly white curriculum and combined with a revolutionary fervor wrought by the political changes and rhetoric of both the civil rights and Black Power movements sweeping the country.[12] Programs, departments, and institutes organized around Black Studies proliferated, in a variety of forms, in America's colleges and universities. Their creation stories were often hotly watched spectacles. Indeed, as argued here, it is the spectacular nature of their beginnings that has, in various ways, continued to define many of these programs and departments, up to the present day.

RISE OF THE BLACK STUDENT MOVEMENT

Perhaps they really should have served that cup of coffee to those Black college students who, on February 1, 1960, ignited the first student protest movement this country had every seen. Perhaps if the employees and manager of that Woolworth's fountain counter had served rather than refused them, the turbulent decade of the 1960s would have become a mere historical footnote rather than a decade of upheaval and unrest throughout the country. Perhaps that one small gesture of serving Black college students would have ushered in, at the dawn of a new decade, a national commitment to eliminate all forms of segregation and exclusion quietly, with resolve. But they didn't serve that cup of coffee, and within weeks, thousands of Black students were arrested and jailed across the South and mid-South, and thousands of white students were joining them in solidarity by picketing and boycotting the Northern headquarters of the chains that were denying service and respect to Black patrons. Within two months a national organization of predominantly Black students formed to coordinate, accelerate, and escalate the challenge to segregation and white supremacy. The first sentence in its founding statement reads: "We affirm the philosophical or religious ideal of nonviolence as the foundation of our purpose, the preposition of our belief, and the manner of our action." That commitment to nonviolence was sorely tested as the civil rights movement joined with the Black Power movement.

In the eight years between the founding of the Student Nonviolent Coordinating Committee (SNCC) and the strident demands for Black Studies, the country lurched reluctantly toward a semblance of racial equality in an atmosphere of assassinations, lynchings, war, urban rebellions, campus upheavals, and police riots. Together, these events tend to obscure one of the central ironies of the decade and of the institutionalization of Black Studies programs: The seed was quiet but determined nonviolence, beginning with Martin Luther King Jr.'s powerful vision of multiracial and harmonious "beloved community," but the harvest consisted of calls for Black Power and societal inclusion for African Americans obtained through what Malcolm X urged should be "any means necessary." As it was, just as the Vietnam War was escalating, the civil rights movement underwent a fundamental change, and Black students were at the center of it. Many of those students were from Black colleges. At the same time, the reality of interracial cooperation in the Black student movement was about to be severely strained.

Moreover, the summer of 1964 was the last in which Black and white students, liberals and radicals, would work together in a spirit of cooperation and nonviolence. Urban "upheaval in Harlem, Rochester, and Watts divided many white liberals and moderates from those white and Black militants who considered the riots legitimate rebellions."[13] In 1965, activist and intellectual Stokely Carmichael helped establish an all-Black political party in Lowndes County, Alabama. During the next spring, he led those who were no longer committed to nonviolence in taking control of the Student Nonviolent Coordinating Committee. Subsequently, whites were expelled from the organization. In the summer of 1966, the cry of "Black Power" was first heard, and Huey Newton and Bobby Seale founded the Black Panther Party in Oakland.[14]

These events marked a rapid erosion of the commitment by Black and some white students associated with the civil rights movement to nonviolence and to interracial political action and had significant consequences for campus protest. Indeed, militancy, unrest, sit-ins, and demands for acknowledgment and justice on Black college campuses increased between 1966 and 1968. In May 1967, students at Jackson State College in Mississippi fought with police for two nights. The National Guard was called, and one person was killed. Sit-ins and student activism by students at Howard University established a pattern that was to be repeated at Black colleges and would spread to Northern campuses as well. On March 19, 1968, a sit-in at Howard University became the first building takeover on a college campus. This event marked the beginning of widespread student activism on college campuses across the country.

By 1969, the Black student revolt calling for Black Studies departments and other demands had reached at least fifty campuses. White colleges, with growing numbers of Black students, were hit particularly hard. This new reality of growth, the influx of nontraditional students, and changing racial dynamics challenged the traditional view of what a university was for and for whom it should be relevant. The university was no longer what could be considered a "cloister" of academics willing to relinquish the temptations of modern life and to look beyond the inevitable cultural and social issues of the day; rather, the university was targeted as a central contributor to the evils of modern society. Indeed, by the end of the 1960s, administrators and faculty members were forced to defend themselves and their institutions from students both Black and white against such charges, and to prove that the education they offered was relevant to modern-day concerns. Race was a central issue. Whereas earlier student activism had generally attacked off-campus targets, by 1968, the protests of Black students were increasingly directed at the university itself.[15] The university, students claimed, had helped to perpetuate Black oppression through its admissions policies, its "white-oriented" curriculum, and its overwhelmingly white teaching staff. Black students found their cultural heritage slighted, or ignored altogether. Their critique of the university intensified in the late 1960s when predominantly white institutions began to admit Black students in larger numbers.

Although attending a predominantly white institution had most likely always been difficult for African American students, those who tended to enroll in such institutions before the 1960s were different from the students who came after. By the late 1960s, political and social events outside of colleges—such as the Vietnam War, the civil rights movement, and the new rhetoric of Black Power—were distracting to students and conflicted with conventional academic pursuits. As Nathan Huggins, a past director of Harvard's African American Studies department, has indicated, in earlier years, "the handful of black students (sometimes as few as one or two in a college as large as

Harvard) fit in either well or badly, but they did so more as individuals who tended to nurse as private matters any hurts or racial slights they may have suffered."[16]

However, as the number of Black college students grew in response to aggressive recruiting efforts and a spate of special programs to allow less traditionally prepared students to obtain an elite education, it became possible for those students to collectively consider for the first time the racism that the colleges and universities were attempting to eliminate. Indeed, given the growth in the numbers of African American students on college campuses, by 1965, what a previous generation of students experienced as private hurts, "often became public grievances and reasons for collective action."[17] As a result, the midcentury growth of American universities in general partially helps to explain the demands and dynamics around the creation of Black Studies programs.

In particular, the issue of relevancy became a catchall phrase for students and captured changes afoot in both the university and the society at large. Black students wanted the university to fund community programs and community learning centers that were relevant to Black students and would provide them an opportunity to tutor Black people not fortunate enough to be in college. They wanted increased levels of financial aid for poor and minority students so that more of America's citizens could participate in the life-changing experience of higher education. In short, they wanted their educations to be useful in ending racism in America. Very often, they also wanted Black studies departments and programs. In response, most American colleges and universities added courses related to Black life, history, and culture, and many attempted to hire more Black faculty and administrators. In a variety of forms, over five hundred programs, departments, and institutes organized around Black Studies proliferated between 1968 and 1971, and their creation often sparked controversy that made the evening news.

Between 1967 and 1975, African American college students, like a noticeable subsection of all college students, became more numerous, vocal, and militant. This is the history out of which Black Studies grew, and as described in some detail in the next chapter, the violent student strike leading to the formation of the country's first African American Studies department took place at San Francisco State College between November of 1968 and March of 1969. The strike came close to anarchy and evolved into a drama featuring the college faculty and students, the mayor of San Francisco, Governor Ronald Reagan, and between two hundred and six hundred members of the riot squad on almost daily alert. As the strike unfolded, the cultural unrest of the period was on full display and was echoed on college campuses around the country. Most tellingly, in April of 1969 at Cornell University, armed Black students occupied and took over Willard Straight Hall. In the course of the occupation, the students made a series of demands that included a new department of African American Studies that should function as an autonomous all-Black college, the hiring of Black faculty and administrators, and the recruitment of poor urban students to the Ivy League university. Cornell's president was in support of beginning a program in Black Studies, but he rejected the idea of its being separatist and all-Black. The standoff ended when the president and students agreed that a department of Afro-American Studies would suffice. In an example of how compelling such incidents were worldwide, the photograph of the students marching out of the building armed with rifles, shotguns, and belts of ammunition slung over their shoulders won the photographer, Steve Starr, a Pulitzer Prize in 1970. Given such high levels of popular interest, the majority of Black Studies programs entered the public consciousness associated with upheaval, militancy, unrest, and violence.

Black militancy and cultural upheaval aside, it is important to note that it was not only large urban universities that recruited Black students and started Black Studies programs. Small, private, liberal arts schools such as Macalester College and Bowdoin College had Black Studies programs by 1970. Moreover, from the late 1960s through 1970, it appeared as though, in one form or another, Black Studies would be widely implemented and accepted on colleges and universities throughout the United States. Indeed, the vast majority of the country's educational institutions added at least a course or two related to African American life, history, and culture, and just as many made great strides in diversifying both their administrative staff and teaching faculty by hiring Black people to fill those positions.

As a result, despite the fact that so much of the creation story of African American Studies revolved around upheaval and violence, it is worth noting that a majority of colleges and universities diversified both their faculties and curricula without significant disruption to their campuses. In fact, most of the institutions that chose to expand their curricula and change the racial makeup of their faculty, like Colby College in Maine, were happy to do so whether or not anyone on campus was asking.

There was, however, often a very different response to demands for a full-fledged program or department of Black Studies, as opposed to a few additional courses. The road became rockier still if the justification for beginning the program or department was perceived to have anything to do with a "new black assertiveness" that "could only antagonize those who held to the ideal of integration and a colorblind system of merit." For many in the nation at large and certainly on college campuses, the insistent demand for Black Studies proved that Black students were "racists who merely wanted to turn an evil on its head." [18] In other words, Black Studies aroused competing tensions whereby Blackness could equal racial cooperation or militancy, but never both simultaneously. Within that context, the questions of political orientation, peaceful racial relations, and

Black Power loomed large. It was precisely these issues that the Ford Foundation had to meet head-on as it endeavored to legitimize Black Studies. It had to choose a particular political side of a contentious debate because history had shown that there was no middle ground. Perhaps surprisingly, the foundation chose to fund Black Studies, arguing that the new field would help white students to better understand Blacks and, by extension, racial relations writ large.

Despite the various factions jockeying for position, only one rationale would come to dominate the field of Black Studies as it assumed its position in academic institutions. Although it clearly did not pioneer the approach, the Ford Foundation wholeheartedly supported an integrationist rationale and refused to fund programs and groups that couched their requests for assistance within the rhetoric of Black Power. Program officers and Board of Trustees members became ever more wary of perceived connections between programs, Black Power ideologies, and the reality of a deepening racial crisis on many campuses. Despite their previous willingness to experiment with alternative strategies, the foundation came to fully believe that the implementation of Black Studies on college campuses should serve as a tool to solve both widely acknowledged historical problems of racial exclusion and contemporary problems of racial integration. Black Studies was not to become a base of power from which nontraditional or experimental solutions for addressing racial conflict could be tried out. As a result of its funding practices, the Ford Foundation helped to craft a rationale for Black Studies that allowed most universities to retain much of what they believed to be inviolate in terms of their organization and autonomy, while simultaneously responding to requests for change coming from within and outside of the university proper.

In short, Ford proposed Black Studies as the solution to a number of institutional problems that colleges and universities were experiencing. It mattered little that the result looked markedly different from the programs many Black students imagined. Nor did it matter that the new strategy appeared to center on the racial education of white students.

In 1969, the tension in Black Studies was between those who believed that it was a means of racial integration and access to increased opportunity, and those who believed that it was tantamount to a revolutionary groundswell capable of overturning the existing social order. Those who believed in racial cooperation would hardly have said that past remedies had been without racial problems, and they certainly would not have exonerated "white administrators for their attitudes and feelings about race." However, they also believed that Blacks "had to succeed, basically, in terms of these imperfect institutions and men, the better to function in the even less perfect world outside" of college. Further, they cautioned, there was not much to be gained, "save the comforts of self-indulgence, by defining oneself outside the system." For them, students and their allies were making a serious mistake in demanding a certain type of autonomy that "would only result in an academic ghetto, an easy way for whites to dismiss blacks—ironically, an invitation to patronizing condescension." Because professional and academic skills, along with exposure to white culture were, they believed, most necessary for Black education, it was imperative that Black Studies not become a stand-alone discipline, and Black students not seek to separate themselves from the mainstream. Indeed, it was the white mainstream that could most benefit from what Black Studies had to offer.[19]

On the other side of the ideological divide, however, many students, activists, and faculty members sought just that type of separation. They believed that Black Studies could mean more than the opportunity for racial integration and heightened sensitivity to an all-encompassing "Negro Problem" on the part of white students and administrators. Such programs, they argued, were a rare opportunity for enacting social change and engendering Black equality within the university, if not the world at large.

Certainly, it was not lost on the students demanding Black Studies programs that African countries were shedding their colonial masters at a quickening pace between 1957, when Ghana first gained independence, and the mid-1960s, when a host of countries followed suit. In a moment of burgeoning Pan-Africanist sentiment, by the late 1960s, some students and activists argued that American Blacks shared a history of colonization with Black people on the African continent, and related their struggle for Black Power and Black Studies to an international struggle to end white supremacy. Such students were not content to view themselves within the narrow confines of American race relations, or to espouse integration as the sole model of racial reform. Indeed, "many Black students at white American universities saw themselves as rebellious subjects of a colonial power" and demanded respect, and a voice in how university funds were to be distributed for financial aid and recruitment and retention of Black students and faculty.[20] They also wanted money for Black Studies programs. Within this context, it was not uncommon for those interested in a more militant organization for Black Studies to co-opt the very language of a colonized country as they discussed what whites could offer them by way of support.

Even for those students, intellectuals, and faculty members content to locate the new field's significance within the boundaries of American culture, there was persistent dissatisfaction with previous efforts to use the issue of race in higher education as a means to an integrationist end. In this instance, their voices were raised in almost direct opposition to the position taken by Black scholars and intellectuals who were most closely aligned with the integrationist aims of the civil rights movement. Those of an earlier generation, such as Kenneth Clark and Bayard

Rustin, argued passionately, persuasively, and vehemently against any type of revolutionary or ideological significance for what was merely a field of study. While that generation railed long and hard against any attempt to organize Black Studies as a separatist field, their arguments were drowned out by the sheer persuasive eloquence of those aligned with more militant sentiments. For example, Eldridge Cleaver, the Black Panther Party's minister of information, argued that Black Studies should be poised to take the lead in an effort to smash the entirety of the white power structure. He believed that Black students on white college campuses were "not reformists, we're not in the movement to reform the curriculum of a given university or a given college or to have a Black Students Union recognized at a given high school. We are revolutionaries, and as revolutionaries, our goal is the transformation of the American social order."[21] His appeal to and for revolution was widely heeded, reproduced, and emulated by African American students in high schools and on college campuses across the country and world. The means of waging revolution was through institutionalizing Black Studies as an independent field capable of delivering institutional power into Black hands, free from the interference of white faculty and administration.

Consequently, for integrationists and Black Power advocates, Black Studies became a means of both addressing and redressing a transnational history of Black exclusion at both the personal and the institutional level. If integrationists saw themselves as needing to fully cooperate with whites in order to right a historical wrong, those interested in Black Power wished to negotiate with whites from a position of power. There was a third constituency that is often confused with those who advocated for Black Power. This group, the cultural nationalists or separatists, assumed that there were two totally separate nations and cultures—one white and the other Black—and there was deep suspicion toward any university effort to assist Black people. Indeed, during the 1969 conference held at Yale University, where McGeorge Bundy declared his intentions to institutionalize the field, a professor named Maulana Karenga clearly articulated that as far as Black activists and students were concerned, there were only three roles for white people and white universities: nonintervention, foreign aid, and civilizing committees. Explaining how these roles would play themselves out in practice, Karenga suggested that nonintervention basically meant autonomy for Black people and for Black Studies on white college campuses; foreign aid meant that whites should provide financial resources for Black people and Black Studies programs; and civilizing "committees should be put into place to civilize white students, faculty and administrators and help them confront and ultimately understand their own racism."[22] Black Studies, according to Karenga and others who shared his views, was not just useful as a means to integrate college campuses, but capable of delivering freedom and power to Black people. The competing aims and understandings of those endeavoring to shape Black Studies in its early years could not have been more different.

McGEORGE BUNDY, THE FORD FOUNDATION, AND BLACK STUDIES

If some Black Studies proponents had a desire to change, transform, challenge, and critique American institutions of higher education, along with ideals around America's democratic process, the Ford Foundation saw itself as transformative in another regard. Although it "actively tried to influence Black Studies programs through strategic grant making," the choices it made as to the types of programs and institutional structures it would support had far-ranging consequences for the future of Black Studies as well as for racial interaction on campuses.[23]

Today, many African American Studies programs and departments remain recruiting tools for a racially diverse student body and faculty, and they can function as symbols of an institution's commitment to racial justice and social reform. Their students and faculty need not, however, be African American themselves, and the cultural interest in a handful of African American personalities and celebrities associated with such programs and departments threatens to overwhelm and undermine a coherent rationale for the discipline, and to obscure the shrinking number of African Americans entering colleges and universities today. The relationship between Black Studies at its inception and Black Studies today is the subject of this book and is held together by a narrative thread situating the role of white philanthropy within the context of race, democratic education, and social reform.

In the third and fourth chapters of this book, the protagonist is McGeorge Bundy, the Ford Foundation's president from 1966 through the end of the 1970s. Those chapters explore his movement through and involvement with Black Power ideologies before settling on the less confrontational integrationist model he would champion as the most useful organizational strategy for African American Studies. Accordingly, they examine both the internal and external struggles and pitfalls he knew his thinking would engender. Chapter 4 examines the thinking and responses of Ford Foundation program officers as they struggled to settle on a grant-making strategy designed to meet Bundy's objectives. These strategies garnered much response from African American students on college campuses, as well as from congressional committees, and that chapter looks at both. Finally, the discussion of Ford and Bundy ends with a discussion of Bundy's role in the Supreme Court's *Bakke* decision, which endorsed the use of racial criteria in university admissions. This was Bundy's final public argument about race relations, and in a magazine article he wrote about the case, he summarized his belief that racial progress could come only through acknowledging that race was central to America's understanding of itself and, to some extent, the rest of the world.[24] Although that argument is true, it has, as the second section shows, produced unexpected consequences for African American Studies.

The last two chapters of *White Money/Black Power* focus on the legacy of the earlier period and explore the conundrum faced by African American Studies today. Overall, they argue that African American Studies as a field is held hostage to its past in two ways, and that the inability to break free from its history has led to its becoming implicated in a cultural landscape where race, and particularly Blackness, means too much and, at the same time, remarkably little. While the early association of African American Studies with a period of political upheaval and unrest continues to undermine its perceived intellectual legitimacy, its early organizational structure in relation to traditional disciplines, and its continued administrative use as a tool for student and faculty recruitment and retention, mark it as an Affirmative Action strategy—and this during a period when such programs are under attack—despite the fact that the students it serves and the faculty it houses are often not African American. In short, the history of African American Studies has produced myriad results. Some are overwhelmingly positive—others are arguably less so.

Within that context, while the Ford Foundation is undeniably one of African American Studies' earliest, biggest, and most enthusiastic financial supporters, it is impossible to ignore the fact that one of the unintended consequences of the strategy it has pursued is that many colleges and universities are hesitant to develop a strategy for moving African American Studies units into the mainstream of the institutional structure. Some of these units occupy the same, often unique status as when they were created, and few that started out as interdepartmental programs have achieved departmental status and, with it, the power and stability of departments. However, when we examine the historical context, it becomes clear that such stability and power were

neither the foundation's goal nor that of most college administrators who rushed to enact such programs during the 1960s
and early 1970s. The real goal was the racial integration and
diversification of college campuses and curricula. African American Studies, as a field or discipline, was merely an expedient
means to a greater end. More than a decade after the 1954
Brown v. Board of Education decision became the law of the
land, the development of African American Studies programs
was seen as a way to move the question of race and public education to the college context. In the 1960s, the enactment of
Black Studies fit nicely with the dominant problem-solving
paradigms in the larger society in regard to race, which favored
programs aimed at the full integration of African Americans
into the larger culture, as an act of democratic and civil reform.
Today, many factors—changing racial demographics; struggles
over the direction, necessity, and viability of affirmative action
programs; and increase in the numbers of students of African
descent from the Caribbean, Africa, and Latin America—have
severely strained the intellectual coherence, cultural significance,
and institutional stability of those programs founded in the late
1960s. *White Money/Black Power* explores how and why this is
the case.

2

BY ANY MEANS NECESSARY

Student Protest and the Birth of Black Studies

"What's gonna happen, now that the king of love is dead?"
Nina Simone

The founding of the nation's first department of Black Studies is the subject of this chapter, as is the student uprising that demanded and won it. The chapter also deals with the strain that the formation of the discipline ultimately placed on ideals of interracial cooperation in higher education. Thus, the focus is on San Francisco State College during the late 1960s, a turbulent time in which many students believed that the institutional acceptance of Black Studies would lead to greater interracial progress and greater flexibility within the academy. Nearly forty years later, with hundreds of Black Studies programs offered in colleges throughout the country, the image that persists is one of angry voices, "nonnegotiable" demands, and raised Black fists. Moreover, not only was San Francisco State the first campus to begin a department of Black Studies, but importantly, the upheaval that preceded that effort persists in far too many minds as a constant theme and meaning attached to the field.

However, we sometimes forget that the thrust for Black Studies was a reflection of the era. Martin Luther King Jr. was murdered in 1968, and even in the years before his murder, race relations were highly charged. Cities around the country were engulfed in what were termed riots, uprisings, and rebellions. The National Guard became an occupying force in first one city, then another. Watts, Newark, Detroit, locales in the East, West, and Midwest were equally prone to urban rebellions. After King's death, many of those same streets smoldered for weeks. At the same time, the war in Vietnam grew increasingly unpopular. Massive demonstrations clogged campuses, streets, and thoroughfares. It was a time characterized by generational conflict, violence, and changing ideals about the meaning of America both at home and abroad. Given that cultural context, it's no wonder that the battle over and for Black Studies resonated so deeply and matters so much.

There is to date no other discipline in the academy so closely aligned with social protest, student activism, and violence as Black Studies, and its emergence and rapid spread surprised many. The events at San Francisco State College did more than introduce the Black Studies programs that now are found on campuses throughout the country; they also pointed poignantly to the perils and promise facing those programs today.

PRELUDE TO A STRIKE

Late in the day on the afternoon of November 5, 1968, a group of Black and Asian, Latino, and Native American "third world" students, from the Black Students Union and the Third World Liberation Front, presented San Francisco State College president Robert R. Smith with a combined list of fifteen non-negotiable demands. The first demand was for the school to immediately establish departments of Ethnic Studies for students from the "third world" and a department of Black Studies for African American students. They demanded no fewer than seventy full-time faculty members, fifty for the departments of Ethnic Studies and twenty for Black Studies. Further, they decreed that the new departments would be solely controlled by the faculty, students, and community groups associated with

their establishment, and that they were to be "free from interference by college administrators, or the statewide Board of
Trustees."[1] In addition, students demanded that the college accept all Black and nonwhite students who applied for admission
in the fall of 1969, regardless of their academic qualifications.
The new departments should be degree-granting, and they could
not be dissolved by the Board of Trustees. Finally, no disciplinary action could be taken against any students, teachers, or administrators who might become involved in the campus strike,
which, they warned, would follow should any of their demands
be rejected.[2]

Students also insisted on the immediate reinstatement of
George Mason Murray, the Black Panther Party's minister of education and a graduate student whom the administration had
suspended for a racially motivated assault on a white editor of
the college's newspaper, the *Daily Gator*. Prior to the attack,
Murray had inflamed California's political leadership and the
college's board of trustees with speeches in which he described
the American flag as "toilet paper," and said that Black students
should carry guns on campus to protect themselves from "racist
administrators." Under orders from State College chancellor
Glenn S. Dumke and the board of trustees, President Smith had
reluctantly (given the campus unrest he was sure would follow)
suspended Murray on November 1.[3]

While he was unwilling to unilaterally agree to all of the students' demands, the president did offer to organize a campuswide convocation for the purpose of discussion. The students
refused and insisted on an immediate answer. President Smith
reluctantly told them that his answer would, under those circumstances, have to be no.

The next day the students launched a strike. A few weeks
later, the faculty joined the students on the picket lines. By the
time the strike ended, almost five months later in March of
1969, San Francisco State not only had a new president, but had
also become the scene of violence "unmatched in the history of

American higher education."[4] For the next several months, the campus became the first "in the nation to be occupied by police on a continuous basis."[5] Indeed, many believed that it was only the daily police presence, estimated to have been between two hundred and six hundred strong, that kept the college open at all. By the end of the strike, more than seven hundred people had been arrested on campus. Over eighty students were injured by police in the process of their arrest, and hundreds more were beaten with police batons, dragged, punched, and slapped, but not arrested.

Violence was not only inflicted on the students but was also perpetrated by them. Thirty-two policemen were injured in altercations with students, and striking students set hundreds of small fires, one of which caused significant damage to the offices of a vice president. Eight bombs made from dynamite were detonated on campus, and on two occasions firebombs were hurled from speeding cars into the home of the assistant to the president, who was particularly vocal in his opposition to the strike and, according to many, hostile both to students and to the idea of forming a department of Black Studies. The damage to buildings and property as a result of the strike ran into tens of thousands of dollars. While there were no deaths directly associated with the strike, the possibility was very real. In mid-February, a white campus guard received severe head injuries when dynamite exploded at the administration building he was guarding. A few weeks later, a nineteen-year-old African American student was partially blinded and maimed when a time bomb—set for the next morning, when the building would have been fully occupied—exploded unexpectedly in the Creative Arts Building. That same night, the police discovered two other bombs, one of them with six sticks of dynamite, in a nearby classroom. It was widely believed that the young man who had been injured had been attempting to set the bombs when one had gone off, although this was never proven.[6]

While the strike began with the demands of a multiracial group of students, at its end, it was almost solely associated with Black students, Black Power, and widespread racial unrest and urban riots. This is in part true because the strike ended when the institution agreed to set up a School of Ethnic Studies and to house the department of Black Studies within it. Although the students of the Third World Liberation Front had demanded the establishment of separate departments of Asian, Latino, and Native American Studies, the only department to receive funding and faculty in the newly established school was Black Studies. Despite the fact that many groups were left out of the final agreement, the Third World Liberation Front claimed victory because they had won a School of Ethnic Studies. The Black Student Union claimed victory because they had won a department of Black Studies. Although not part of the decision-making or negotiation committee who formally submitted the list of student demands, the predominantly white Students for a Democratic Society (SDS) also claimed victory. They had participated in a strike against educational racism, one of their main issues, and had forced the administration to respond. In short, as far as students were concerned, there was widespread satisfaction with the conclusion of the strike. However, at the same time, the multiracial nature of the student alliance and the coherent analysis of the role of racial integration in ending social injustice had both changed significantly by the strike's end, and the role of striking white students in particular was a consistent source of discussion and contention. Nonetheless, the strike and all those who participated in it were responsible for the advent of Black Studies.

SAN FRANCISCO STATE: AN UNLIKELY PLACE FOR A REVOLUTION

San Francisco State College sits in the midst of an unremarkable and peaceful suburban community far from the tourist attractions that so frequently draw visitors to the city. During the late 1960s, although still a college, San Francisco State was as large as many universities, with 18,000 undergraduates. It offered sixty-three types of bachelor's degree programs, forty-four master's degree programs, and a doctorate in education.[7] It was always predominantly a commuter campus whose students arrived from all over the San Francisco Bay area by car or bus. Most of those students came from the working class; indeed, in 1968, 80 percent of the students worked to pay their way through school and came from predominantly lower middle-class, poor, and working-class communities. Their counterparts at the nearby Berkeley campus of the University of California were rarely forced to juggle the world of work with their academic pursuits. Yet the state spent six dollars to educate each student attending college in the UC system, and less than two dollars on the education of those attending San Francisco State College—a fact not lost on activist students. This glaring disparity reinforced their view that education and educational institutions were engaged in a process of oppressing and disenfranchising students who were not from the middle class, not already socially and economically secure. By 1968, there were racial concerns about the student body at San Francisco State as well as class concerns.[8]

In 1960, 12 percent of the students at San Francisco State College were African American. By 1968, Black enrollment had dropped to 3 percent, in part as a result of the military draft into the war in Vietnam, and in part as a result of a system of "tracking" Black and poor students into schools for vocational education, as opposed to the liberal arts. Unlike many other colleges and universities in the country in 1968, San Francisco State College experienced a growth in calls for Black Studies and in the rhetoric of Black militancy, as the numbers of Black students shrank. If Black and poor students could not attend the state colleges specifically established to include them, many students believed that they needed no further proof of the necessity for social change. The precipitous decline in enrollment of Black students partly explains the multiracial coalition of students who would join together in a student strike. Within that context, students viewed the formation of a Black Studies department as a tangible remedy for what many believed was an American educational system and culture bent on exclusion and hostile to economic and racial integration.[9]

Still, San Francisco State was an unlikely place for an ugly, protracted strike, and the presence or absence of Black students does not itself explain the events that took place on the campus during that four-month period. San Francisco was then and remains a sophisticated and cosmopolitan city, always viewed as tolerant and liberal; it surprised many that such a devastating strike occurred there. This was true for the campus as well. Indeed, in the years preceding the strike, many hailed San Francisco State as an innovative, liberal institution that had a history of treating students with respect and understanding. It also had a reputation as a peaceful campus where cooperation and understanding between students, faculty, and administrators flourished. The institution had avoided the student protest and campus shutdown concerning free speech that had so troubled UC Berkeley in 1964, and again in 1966. When a reporter asked students at San Francisco State if they intended to join in the student protests at Berkeley, one answered, "No. Why should we? We have free speech and we are treated like adults."[10] Even the Kerner Commission Report on the San Francisco State College strike observed that students on other college campuses across the country began by the mid-1960s to agitate to convert their own campuses into the kind of college that San Francisco State already was.

In addition, the institution had established a tradition of pedagogical experimentation and educational innovation. In 1965, despite budgetary constraints and the active disapproval of some trustees and politicians, the administration endorsed and encouraged students to develop and implement the first "experimental" college, where students designed courses and taught other students, as well as hired the professors. Although such a development troubled some, the new college was peacefully instituted. There were other areas as well in which San Francisco State College had assumed a leadership role. The first Black Student Union (BSU) in the country was founded at San Francisco State in March of 1966, and in 1968 students founded and the college fully funded the Third World Liberation Front, another first.[11]

Moreover, while it was not the first college to offer courses related to Black Studies, by 1968 San Francisco State already offered a number of them, primarily in history and literature, and it was aggressively seeking funding for teaching even more such courses, although it did not have an academic department devoted to them. The college also employed three teachers and six administrators who were African American. As a result of what they saw as their goodwill, forward-looking nature, and willingness to experiment and compromise, college administrators were more than puzzled and a bit angry when students began to brand them as "racists" and "enemies of the people" intent on oppressing students, maintaining the status quo, and upholding white supremacy. Nor could they understand the demands for students to have a far greater role in defining the mission and the function of the institution as a whole. Many administrators felt that they had been doing exactly that.[12]

However, while individual administrators may not have understood the cultural shifts they were up against, they were witnessing at San Francisco State overall changes beginning to take place on college campuses all over the country. These were a part of the burgeoning student protest movement that began to sweep the nation at the dawn of the decade. That movement opposed racial inequity and the war in Vietnam. Between those two anchors was a growing distrust of and antagonism toward institutions of higher learning, because they appeared to support and advance both of the issues against which the movement defined itself. By 1968, the Student Nonviolent Coordinating Committee (SNCC) had left college campuses for intensive voter registration and organizing work in the rural South, and had largely abandoned its philosophy of nonviolence in the face of the ongoing reign of terror in the region. Although it supported this work, the Students for a Democratic Society (SDS) remained principally on the campuses and at the center of calls for a re-organization of academic priorities. The role of the SDS in the strike, however, would become and remain a source of contention at the college and between Black and white students across the country.

THE WHITE STUDENT PROTEST MOVEMENT:
PORT HURON STATEMENT

Students for a Democratic Society was established in 1959 as a radical student group for the children of members of both the Communist and Socialist Parties—children who were often referred to as "red diaper babies." It developed out of the youth branch of an older socialist educational organization, the League for Industrial Democracy. The organization's founders viewed college campuses and the white middle-class students inhabiting them as keys to unlocking widespread cultural change and bringing about social equality in America. In their initial statement, they boldly announced, "We are people of this generation, bred in at least modest comfort, housed now in universities, looking uncomfortably to the world we inherit."[13] After declaring their generation and class, they went further. "Our comfort was penetrated by events too troubling to dismiss. First, the permeating and victimizing fact of human degradation, symbolized by the Southern struggle against racial bigotry, compelled most of us from silence to activism. The declaration 'all men are created equal...' rang hollow before the facts of Negro life in the South and the big cities of the North."[14] Far from imagining that the views they held were in conflict with America's founding doctrine, in their initial conversations the organization's founders came to believe that America had merely lost its way, that ideals of democracy, freedom, and equality had become mythic, remote possibilities. However, they believed that such ideals could be reclaimed, and they declared that the effort to bring about the types of societal and political change they sought would "involve national efforts at university reform by an alliance of students and faculty."[15]

Influenced by the movement led by the Black college students in the Student Nonviolent Coordinating Committee, the SDS held its first official meeting in April of 1960, a few weeks after SNCC's founding meeting at Shaw University in Raleigh, North Carolina. At SDS's initial meeting, in Ann Arbor, Michigan, they crafted what would become their political manifesto, the Port Huron Statement. In large part, the document was written by Tom Hayden, a twenty-two-year-old former editor of the student newspaper at the University of Michigan, who would later gain notoriety for his political views about the Vietnam War, his time in Congress, and his marriage to the actress Jane Fonda. Adopted by the organization in 1962, the document criticized the whole of the American political system for its inability to achieve international peace, and for failing to effectively address and solve the social ills of racism, materialism, militarism, poverty, and exploitation. As an antidote, the statement declared, middle-class white students had to wrest control of the educational process from the administrative bureaucracy and "make fraternal and functional contact with allies in labor, civil rights, and other liberal forces outside the campus. They must import major public issues into the curriculum   research and teaching on problems of war and peace is an outstanding example. They must make debate and controversy, not dull pedantic cant, the common style for educational life. They must consciously build a base for their assault upon the loci of power."[16] The statement went on to call for a fully "participatory democracy" that would empower citizens to make the political decisions then decided by politicians. Although their thinking would change, at its outset, the group believed that their movement would be nonviolent, along the lines Martin Luther King's movement for civil rights. This student-based movement, occurring on college campuses, they believed, could transform the United States.

In an effort to model the kind of behavior and commitment they called for from others, between 1963 and 1964 many SDS members participated in the civil rights movement, often taking time off from school in order to travel south to join the voter registration efforts spearheaded by SNCC. Those were particularly brutal years. In September of 1963, four little girls, Cynthia Wesley, Addie Mae Collins, Denise McNair, and Carole Robertson were killed when a bomb, planted by white racists, exploded at the Sixteenth Street Baptist Church in Birmingham, Alabama. A few months before, state NAACP chief Medgar Evers was assassinated outside his home in Jackson, Mississippi. In the summer of 1964, three civil rights workers—James Chaney, Andrew Goodman and Michael (Mickey) Schwerner—were brutally murdered and mutilated in the Mississippi delta while attempting to register African American voters for the upcoming election. Weary of burying their friends and supporters, by the close of 1964 both SNCC and SDS had grown disillusioned with the tactics of nonviolence, and both openly called for armed self-defense and, later, revolution.

The Southern civil rights movement not only influenced the formation of SDS, it also influenced another highly politicized campus disruption, the Berkeley Free Speech Movement, led by Mario Savio. Fresh from the Mississippi delta, where he'd spent the summer of 1964 organizing voter registration drives, Savio told students in one speech: "Last summer I went to Mississippi to join the struggle there for civil rights. This fall I am engaged in another phase of the same struggle, this time in Berkeley."[17] Drawing a connection between his work with SNCC and his organizing at Berkeley, he said, "In Mississippi an autocratic and powerful minority rules, through organized violence to suppress the vast, virtually powerless majority. In California, the privileged minority manipulates the university bureaucracy to suppress the students' political expression." He urged the students of his generation to fight against what he termed the educational-corporate machine, saying, "There is a time when the operation of the machine becomes so odious, makes you so sick to heart that... you've got to put your bodies upon the gears and upon the wheels, upon the levers, upon all the apparatus, and you've got to make it stop. And you've got to indicate to the people who run it, to the people who own it, that unless you're free, the machine will be prevented from working at all."[18] The Free Speech Movement erupted as a reaction against the heavy-handed attempts by Berkeley officials, under pressure by prominent conservatives, to prevent students from collecting donations and recruiting other students for organizing work in the segregated South. Official overreaction to mild student resistance led to massive sit-ins and occupation of the university's administration building. The arrests of over five hundred demonstrators led to several weeks of even more massive demonstrations and a strike by nearly 70 percent of the Berkeley student body.

The campus activism heralded by SNCC, SDS, and the Berkeley Free Speech Movement soon spread to colleges and universities all over the United States. Even students who never joined SDS heeded its call to action:

In each community we must look within the university and act with confidence that we can be powerful.... As students for a democratic society, we are committed to stimulating this kind of social movement, this kind of vision and program in campus and community across the country. If we appear to seek the unattainable, as it has been said, then let it be known that we do so to avoid the unimaginable.[19]

In 1968, about forty thousand students on nearly a hundred campuses across the country demonstrated against the Vietnam War and linked their concerns about the war to charges of racism aimed at what they viewed as racist treatment of the Vietnamese and African Americans both in the military and at home. Protest against one often became protest against the other. At Columbia University, an SDS-led antiracist demonstration against the university's plans to demolish a housing complex in Morningside Park (which separated the university from Harlem) and erect a gymnasium became a protest against the war. The SDS took over the administration building, as well as several other university buildings, and nearly a thousand angry students set up barricades and established what they termed "revolutionary communes" behind them. When the police stormed the buildings and randomly brutalized the occupying students, a majority of students at Columbia joined in a boycott of classes that shut down the university. In addressing the protesters at Columbia about the university's plans to demolish housing occupied by African Americans and build space for the university, Black Panther leader H. Rap Brown urged protesters to stand strong and see themselves as in charge: "If they build the first story, blow it up. If they sneak back at night and build three stories, burn it down. And if they get nine stories built, it's yours. Take it over, and maybe we'll let them in on the weekends."[20]

Despite the overlap in issues impacting Black and white students, and the spirit of cooperation between the two groups, increasingly, the student protest movement would splinter into causes deemed Black or white, and the role of white student groups was, by the fall of 1968, hotly contested. At San Francisco State, the SDS-led student protest movement combined with the growing sense of power on the part of Black student groups, and the whole was exacerbated by the instability of leadership at the campus. Initially, it was the responsibility of one man, President Summerskill, the new head of San Francisco State, to maintain order in the midst of increasingly complex levels of chaos and escalating tendencies toward violence. When he first came to the campus in 1966, it was with an overwhelming sense of optimism about what was possible and how much could be accomplished between administrators and students, if both showed a sense of respect and openness. By the time he resigned in February of 1968, he had run afoul of not just the board of trustees, but the state's popular new Governor, Ronald Reagan. Indeed, in leaving his position, he did not mention the student strike, racial disturbances, or the fact that a majority of the board of trustees had earmarked him for dismissal due to what they believed was his failure to adequately deal with the increasing level of violent unrest on the campus. Instead, he chalked his departure up to the administration of Ronald Reagan, which he believed was "eroding by political interference and financial starvation" the public trust in the institution's teachers and administrators. Whatever the reason for his short tenure at the institution, his departure was an unhappy end to what had begun as a hopeful appointment.[21]

THE STRIKE IN BLACK AND WHITE

I went to San Francisco State to be an educational leader. That was my intention. But the Vietnam War was on and the students hated the war. It was also the time when black people decided to seize equity in America. Then, partly in response, the people of California elected a conservative governor and the fight was on. My life in San Francisco was a desperate attempt to keep the radicals and the reactionaries from each other's throats.[22]

During his brief tenure at San Francisco State, Summerskill was not only confronted by radical students but by the college's conservative students, who felt that they had long been ignored by both the student government and college administration. They began to bring pressure from the other side of the political spectrum and put together a coalition that won the student government election against a Black opponent in the spring of 1967. Their first official act was to reduce the hoped-for appropriations for the experimental college. In a sign of the chaos quickly taking over the campus, conservative students, believing that white hippies and Black militants were being given far too much consideration, took over the administration building. The police were called in to remove them after a nine-hour sit-in demonstration during which approximately four hundred politically conservative students protested against: the end of Air Force ROTC on campus, programs to admit four hundred working-class Black students in the fall semester, and the hiring of nine minority faculty members to help the minority students. Twenty-six persons were arrested.[23]

In May of 1967, the new student government moved against the Black Student Union, charging it with reverse racism, misuse of student funds, and threats of violence. These accusations led the board of trustees to send a committee to investigate the BSU and related student financial affairs at San Francisco State. The committee found that there was not enough evidence to support the charges, but recommended that the college tighten its student disciplinary procedures and fiscal controls.[24] Although no wrongdoing had been found, conservative white students continued to challenge the idea that courses organized around Black Studies should receive support. In October, the Carnegie Corporation invited the college to apply for funds to develop programs for teaching Black history, art, and culture. James Vaszko, the editor of the campus newspaper, *The Golden Gater,* wrote an editorial to the Carnegie Corporation asking the foundation to cease any plans they might have to grant money to the college's "service programs," including any funds to support Black students.

It was not the first article to enrage the Black students on the campus, who saw a pattern of racist humor and racist attacks in the campus paper. They were further insulted at the paper's persistence in referring to the boxing champion Muhammad Ali as Cassius Clay. This last, the students claimed, was the height of disrespect, since a person should be able to decide the name by which he is be called.[25] On November 6, 1967, over one dozen members of the BSU went to the newspaper offices with a folder containing the offensive articles that had recently run in the newspaper. The visit turned into a physical assault against Vaszko and random white members of the paper's staff, and the incident would become a contributing factor to the strike that began almost one year later.

BSU president Jimmy Garrett remembered the event:

We were going to see three people that day. We were going to see the editor of the *Gater,* the chairman of the school of education and the dean of students. All on the same question, racism. . . . This was about some different kinds of racist things we thought they were pulling, so we went to talk to them . . . about Muhammad Ali and a series of things. So one of the things we brought with us was a folder full of the different articles that we had documented and Xeroxed. We went up there and then the white boy [Vaszko] said some things, and he got hit in the mouth. He didn't get hurt, which is what he should have done.[26]

Vaszko, however, offered a different story. According to the article printed in the *Gater* the next morning, when the fifteen members of the BSU arrived, five went into the office occupied by Vaszko, while the rest waited outside. According to Vaszko, he was on the phone when they arrived. He recalled saying, "I'll be with you in a second." In response, one of the BSU members "ripped the phone from my hands and began beating me with it." He fell to the floor where, he recalled, he was kicked repeatedly.[27] Meanwhile, when the white staff members heard the commotion and tried to enter the office, they were stopped by the BSU members. By all accounts, what can only be described as a free-swinging melee ensued. One of the few students clearly visible in the photographs taken of the incident by the newspaper's photographer was George Mason Murray, coordinator of the BSU-run urban tutorial program and a graduate student who held a part-time teaching post in the English department.

A few days after the incident, the BSU students who were involved in the incident turned themselves in rather than risk arrest. Murray and six others were booked on felony charges and suspended. The incident led to a heightened rhetoric of violence and retribution. The students offered no apology. At a Fresno State College rally following his suspension, Murray told listeners that, "We are slaves, and the only way to become free is to kill all the slave masters."[28] One BSU member, Jerry Varnado, when asked if the physical attack at the *Gater* office was a new aspect of their political strategy, answered, "You want to talk about violence. All right, let's talk about Vietnam." He proceeded to list statistics showing the disproportionate number of nonwhite troops killed there.[29] When BSU president Jimmy Garrett was asked about the organization's position on the attack of the editor, he replied:

We had reached a point where we took a move from rhetoric to the element of action, and there was no return.

We already had an atmosphere of violence. But the violence was psychological. The question of violence is a dual question, because violence has been committed against us ever since we had been on campus. We just didn't arbitrarily jump on white folks, because if we had wanted to do it, we could have done that every day of the week.[30]

In response to an appeal filed by the suspended students, the college's Board of Appeals and Review held closed hearings on December 6. Sympathetic students picketed outside. The demonstration united students with a wide variety of grievances. There were the Black students of the BSU, urban high-school students, and antiwar white students. According to Summerskill, the protest:

Brought together for the first time various radical elements on the campus with their supporters from a number of Bay Area communities.... We have never been confronted by this group of people... Black Student Union people by and large simply do not talk to SDS antiwar people but this time, because suspensions were involved, they were talking and acting in unison.[31]

The first of many student takeovers happened that day. "School is closed!" chanted the crowds. Several hundred Black and white protestors surged up the steps to the administration building and through the glass door, with media people and photographers trailing them. Summerskill was in his office with representatives of the San Francisco Police Department, and a few buildings away, two hundred policemen waited for the signal to enter the melee. President Summerskill and his police advisers decided to close the campus rather than risk bringing in the police. Fistfights broke out between students and nonstudents, although the crowd dispersed without further incident after about three hours. The suspensions, which had been lifted initially, were reinstated, then lifted and reinstated a number of times between December of 1967 and the beginning of the strike almost a year later.

By February 1968, the mounting campus tensions led Dr. Summerskill to resign, effective September 1. However, on May 25, the chancellor of California's state colleges, Glenn Dumke, demanded Summerskill's immediate resignation and refused to wait for the beginning of the new academic year. This reaction was precipitated by Summerskill's reluctance to call in the police to forcibly put down what was described as a "small group of students" who had taken over the administration building three days before, following a speech by Black Panther Party minister of defense Bobby Seale. In a faculty resolution put forward in support of Summerskill, his reluctance to meet student protest with force was hailed as an embrace of the nonviolent social strategies of Martin Luther King Jr., but faculty support was no match for the continuing criticism by Governor Reagan, and Summerskill was terminated.[32]

It would be the next president who would preside over much of the campuswide strike to come, although he did take steps to avert it. Dr. Robert Smith was a professor of education. One of his first acts as president was to agree to the creation of a department of Black Studies and to appoint Dr. Nathan Hare to lead it. Despite what would appear to have been a victory, for the students and Dr. Smith alike, the students rejected the offer because the new department did not have the level of autonomy they demanded. Then, shortly after he assumed his new office, Smith was pressured to suspend George Murray, who had been rehired just days before. But Murray had recently returned from a trip to Cuba, where he had repeated his assertion that Black students in the United States ought to begin carrying guns on campus in order to protect themselves from racist administrators. As late as September 29, the new president was quoted in an article in the *New York Times* as saying that "odds [were] against" his asking for Murray's resignation, or suspending him. But the trustees disagreed, and forced the recently installed president to suspend George Murray on October 31, although Murray was still eligible to collect his full salary of $282 per month.[33] As soon as the suspension was announced, the Black Student Union called for a student strike.

More than a hundred African American students and a handful of sympathizers burst into classrooms and demanded that teachers and students alike support the strike. Faculty who declined were chased from the buildings, and a number of fights broke out between students who supported the strike and those who did not. Several windows were broken, one by a flying typewriter, and the students forced a number of news photographers to empty their cameras of film. By the time the police tactical squad arrived on campus, all of the students had left the premises, and there were no arrests that day. It was a prelude to the upheaval that was to come.[34]

Initially, student support for the strike was tepid, but by the middle of November, the atmosphere had changed. Black, white, and brown students increasingly viewed the administration's actions as racist and authoritarian, and the administration itself as weak, controlled by conservative and callous politicians in Sacramento and conservative, rich, white trustees in Los Angeles. They felt that Murray's suspension illustrated the racism and authoritarianism found not only on college campuses but in the larger society. There was no further room for debate, as one informational leaflet made clear in its warning to students inclined to cross the picket lines and attend classes: "By crossing the picket line you have consciously or not put yourself in a position against the strike of the BSU-TWLF. This is a strike against racism that recognizes the right of the oppressed Third World people to self-determination by any means necessary. By crossing the line you have made your choice—there is no middle ground."[35] Concerning the violent tactics by then engulfing the strike, one Black student leader asserted, "People accuse you of being violent when you shove a man off your foot after you've asked him to please stop standing on your toe. And the myth that this is violence is a myth and has no basis in fact. A cornered mouse will eventually do something in his defense, and that is the frustrating position that poor people are always put into, which inevitably leads to some kind of aggression in self-defense."[36] Black community leaders, political leaders, and students then joined the protests in earnest. At that point, the issue the students were most intent upon resolving was the issue of educational racism, and they believed that the institutionalization of Black Studies was the way to bring about meaningful change. The head of the BSU told reporters that "Black people's lives are built on a different set of experiences from white folks. You see this historically in the persecution black people have undergone in this country."[37] George Murray went on to add, "The struggle at San Francisco State and the BSUs throughout the State is a struggle for the seizure of power and the implementation of one primary point, which is the determination of our destiny educationally, politically, socially and economically. In other words, we are struggling for freedom and the goal is the seizure of power to bring about that freedom."[38]

While many agreed that whites, moderate and radical, played a large and supportive role in the strike, all generally conceded that they were largely absent at the level of planning and strategy. This was not their choice. In the early days of the strike, the picket lines at the main college entrance were staffed almost entirely by white students and faculty, and far more white students clashed with the police at whom they hurled both rocks and insults. Indeed, of the 731 total arrests associated with the strike, over 650 involved white students. However, early on, members of the BSU and the Third World Liberation Front assumed the lead role in planning and strategy. This did not sit well with the members of the two most radical white student groups on campus, the SDS and the Progressive Labor Party, who had numerous disagreements with other predominantly white student groups and with groups composed of students of color. One issue of contention was SDS's widespread practice of taking over and occupying the administration buildings on college campuses, a practice that often led to confrontations with the police. "We thought it was irrelevant," Jimmy Garrett, explained. He went on to add that, concerning the strike at SFS, "We didn't think the white students should lead anything."[39]

Black student leaders at other campuses also criticized some of tactics of SDS-led demonstrations. Speaking to members of the BSU and the Third World Liberation Front at San Francisco State in November of 1967, Stokely Carmichael—the Black student leader who had headed SNCC when, by a narrow vote, it had expelled its white staff people—told those gathered that he thought the white student groups should remain in the background of the struggle at the college:

> You're now beginning to challenge real attitudes. Who has the right to hire and to fire. Not even the white student movement in the height of its movement at Columbia was able to do this. Because they held the buildings for a few days, then they gave up, but they had no clear victories. You read about Mark Rudd [the SDS student leader at Columbia], Yeah, he's sho' nuff bad. But he ain't got nothing to show for his badness. And I don't think we can afford that, because we're not in the same position as white students. They have the luxury of being militant or radical or revolutionary. For us, it is a necessity. We have no other out.[40]

Elements of this position continued to appear in BSU statements, especially those suggesting that the seizure of college buildings was pointless. Carmichael articulated another element of BSU strategy when he told his audience, "When you fight, you depend only upon yourselves, nobody else.... That's black people, and then that's people of color outside of this circle. But you look upon yourself."[41] In short, the BSU viewed SDS as having fixed ideas about class struggle and student power that had little to do with what they saw as the key issue of racism. They believed that the SDS could afford to protest against relatively minor issues, like cafeteria food, since its individual members could always disappear back into white society and privilege. The Black students were firm: while white groups were welcome to participate, their participation could not be at the level of decision making, leadership, or strategy.

SDS leaders argued that the main issues of the strike were racism and the class structure of the university, and that violence and social unrest were viable strategies for effecting change in both. In a pamphlet issued by the White Students' Strike Committee, SDS argued that racism was a tool of the ruling class that affected all oppressed people—including white students. They agreed, however, to limit their role in the strike. As one striking student interpreted the compromise, "The word is, that if you want to throw rocks or plant bombs, that's OK, as long as you don't try to change the issues or make new demands."[42]

On November 13, following a week of escalating violence and a faculty vote that he do so, President Smith suspended classes indefinitely. The previous week had seen the detonation of a bomb backstage of the college's 750-seat main auditorium, causing minor damage. The following week, with the campus still closed, President Smith informed Governor Reagan and the board of trustees that he would need at least one more week to negotiate with striking students and create an atmosphere wherein the negotiating could take place without an accompanying "show of force." The trustees responded by calling an emergency meeting in which they demanded that he reopen the institution immediately and vowed that there would be "no negotiation, arbitration or concession" to either the students or the faculty. At that same meeting, a staff representative demanded a "definite, realistic plan of protection" to ensure that the college's staff would be safe from "vandals, ruffians, anarchists and amateur demolition squads." The trustees promised that the campus would be reopened by the next day and that force would be used if necessary. Dr. Smith resigned a few days later, on November 26, 1968.[43]

Appointed as the acting president was Dr. S. I. Hayakawa, a noted semanticist. The word most often used to describe President Hayakawa is "authoritarian." His administration, he said on the day he was appointed, would not accept change through intimidation. He went on to add that the campus was open for "sensible students and faculty" and ended by saying that "unsensible ones can leave."[44] If students marched on the administration building, then he would see to it that the San Francisco police would be there to meet them. When the new acting president arrived on campus on December 2, the first day that classes were to be held, he found himself immediately surrounded by demonstrators shouting, "On Strike, Shut it Down!" Instead of retreating into a nearby building, Hayakawa climbed onto a campus-owned truck equipped with a public address system mounted on its bed. The students shouted him down and ripped out the microphone wires. Hayakawa then began to try to distribute copies of a statement he had prepared. Someone shoved him and he shoved back, screaming, "Don't you touch me!" Asked how he felt about having an altercation greet him in his new role, he answered that he was ready for it, even "exhilarated." George Murray, whose suspension was one of the causes of the strike, was on hand to greet President Hayakawa as well. Speaking from the steps of the administration building, he told demonstrating students that, "It is a historic moment. The people are participating in an attempt to seize power. Hayakawa has no authority to come in and usurp the power of the people." When asked what he thought about these statements, Hayakawa responded that as a result of Murray's speech, he would institute new disciplinary action against him.[45]

Despite his tough talk and memorable first day on the job, the violence did not abate. Indeed it intensified, and Hayakawa's reliance on San Francisco's police force led to injury and bloodshed. On December 3, the day after he took office, "Bloody Tuesday" occurred. It began when a demonstrator, standing in front of the building where business and social science classes were held, shouted, "This is one of the most racist buildings on campus. We're going to shut it down." Policemen responded quickly, attacking a group of roughly three hundred students with clubs. Nearly a thousand students, most of them white, joined the melee. As reporters watched, police swinging clubs beat hundreds of protesters to the ground, forcing the students and faculty to break up furniture and use it as clubs against the police.

Unable to resolve the conflict in any other way, college administrators agreed to return to the bargaining table, although the final resolution would take some time. At issue for the students was the fact that, despite what appeared to have been a real victory with President Smith agreeing to begin a department of Black Studies, President Hayakawa had fired the department's first chair, Nathan Hare, soon after assuming office, and had refused to rehire either Hare or George Murray.[46] On March 21, 1969, the strike ended. While this was clearly a victory, the drama surrounding the new program did not really end there. In June of 1969, four of six Black administrators resigned, charging Hayakawa with racism. By Christmas of that year, President Hayakawa accused the department of maintaining a "reign of terror" and pledged to disband it. On March 3, 1970, almost a year after the day of the strike's end, he fired the entire Black Studies faculty, ostensibly because the department had not submitted its hiring, retention, and tenure committee reports until an hour before the deadline. Although the department reopened a few months later under new leadership, its background of campus upheaval is still what people remember.[47]

In many ways, the battle for Black Studies was won on the day that the strike ended at San Francisco State. Even years later, however, the battle was still being waged, and before it was over, another incident centering on Black Studies would rock a college campus on the other side of the country.

At San Francisco State, the issue was the meaning of higher education, in relation to a white student protest movement and a growing rhetoric of Black self-determination and self-defense, but the conflict at Cornell was over the treatment of Black students who had been recruited in the interests of diversity. If the world took note of San Francisco State because of the duration of the strike and the violence involved, at Cornell University, the takeover of a campus building, accompanied by demands for a Black Studies department, was newsworthy because this institution was a member of the Ivy League. And unlike the students at San Francisco State, Cornell students demanded Black Studies with guns in hand and readily visible for all to see. As a result, the call for Black Studies at that institution, as at San Francisco State, was associated with violence—but it galvanized the country in a very different manner.

CORNELL UNIVERSITY

Early Saturday morning, April 19, 1969, over one hundred of the three hundred African American students attending Cornell University took over and occupied Willard Straight Hall. By midafternoon, guns had been brought into the building. The photographic images of armed African American students on an Ivy League campus traveled through phone lines and appeared in numerous media outlets around the world. In a very real sense, the image of African American students marching across Cornell's campus with rifles resting lightly at their hips, their dark faces gazing out from under neatly styled Afros, came to define both the promise and perils of integration. They were images of Black Power's rhetoric come to life and symbolized the societal face of Black nationalism, while simultaneously speaking about a brewing cultural confrontation over what it was America owed its citizens of African descent.

The takeover was the culmination of a two-year campaign to force Cornell to open a college, department, or center of Black Studies on the campus. The specific event that led to the confrontation was spurred by a faculty-student judicial board's decision to punish Black students for a disruptive protest the previous December. There was also a cross-burning at a Black women's dorm that most Black students believed was the work of whites.[48] It is important to note that there has been some suggestion by students involved in the occupation that the cross-burning may have actually been carried out by a group of Black students who wanted to ignite the atmosphere on campus. In any case, after white students briefly broke into Willard Straight Hall and the campus police did nothing to stop them, the Black students armed themselves.[49]

While the public issue was the fact of Black students with guns taking over a campus building, the larger context had to do with a special program the university had instituted to try to recruit inner-city Black students to the campus. Begun in 1963 and called the Committee on Disadvantaged Students, it was renamed the Committee on Special Educational Projects (COSEP) in 1965. Its purpose was to "recommend and initiate programs for students who have been disadvantaged by their cultural, economic, and educational environments."[50] Although not necessarily only for Black students, in practice, the program predominantly functioned as a means to bring Black students to the campus. It is interesting to note that John Summerskill, former president of San Francisco State College, was in charge of the program for increasing minority enrollment at Cornell, while a professor at that institution. Since it was primarily a fundraising and recruitment tool, in the beginning, no one considered Black Studies as part of the committee's mandate. However, committee members, many of whom were active in the civil rights movement, wanted something more radical to take place; they began to actively recruit urban Black students to Cornell and to offer verbal support for the idea of a Black Studies department, to help those students feel more comfortable.

As a result, the specific event leading to the armed confrontation on Cornell's campus grew out of a yearlong struggle about what groups of African American students saw as their mistreatment, but the larger issues spoke to the space for and place of African American students at desegregated and predominantly white college campuses. Administrators hoped that the establishment of African American Studies programs and departments would ameliorate racial tensions on their campuses and in the country at large. It was seen as a solution for myriad problems. At the same time, altruism alone does not fully explain the widespread and enthusiastic response to calls for the formation of such programs. No fewer than three hundred would be instituted between 1968 and 1971, and many were begun on campuses where students had not actually expressed an interest. While the history of Black studies at San Francisco State and Cornell makes clear why violence and social appeasement are so often associated with Black Studies, what is less clear is why, given the widespread mistrust of Black Studies as a field, many institutions chose to implement it so rapidly.

At San Francisco State, Black Studies was seen as a means of reforming higher education, but that idea got hopelessly lost as colleges and universities rushed to implement Black Studies programs. Administrators turned a blind eye to the underlying issues in which the students were interested, and went in another direction entirely. The next chapter argues that, if McGeorge Bundy and The Ford Foundation had not crafted a strategy to address such concerns and offer solutions to the problems of campus administrators, the field might never have survived beyond that initial rush.

3

NATION BUILDING IN THE BELLY OF THE BEAST

In August of 1966 when the Ford Foundation's new president, McGeorge Bundy, announced that solving America's racial troubles would define his presidency, he had only been in his new job for a few months. However, given the fact that at his first meeting with Ford's board of trustees, he had secured their backing to make race—and more particularly, the "Negro Problem"—the foundation's priority, it is not surprising that he would publicly voice his plans so soon after taking charge of the organization.[1] At the time, the student strike at San Francisco State was still on a distant horizon, and the civil rights movement was just beginning to publicly respond to Black and white students who were dissatisfied with its strategy of nonviolence. At the same time, America's cities seemed to many to be locked in a cycle of upheaval and violence. Nineteen sixty-six saw the third summer of urban conflict. In addition, the brand-new ideology of Black Power, adopted by Black students and activists such as Stokely Carmichael, convinced many, both Black and white, that race relations in the country would be rocky for some time to come. It is, then, somewhat understandable that, at a National Urban League dinner in 1966, Bundy declared his intention to focus a great deal of time, money, and attention on solving America's problems with race. Indeed, he told the audience that he and Ford believed "that full equality for all American Negroes is now the most urgent domestic concern of the country.... If the ghetto pulls the central city down...if bad schools drive out good parents of all colors; if slums beget slums and hatred hate...then we shall know a time when the shame of Lincoln Steffens's cities will seem a tale of Pollyanna."[2]

Given the fact that the country was engaged in the Vietnam War, his belief that African Americans were the most pressing concern for the country must certainly have surprised at least a few. However, this was not a speech or commitment that he made lightly. Bundy made clear that he believed, "That a wider and deeper and stronger effort among white leaders is needed so that the white American can see the problem as it really is, and recognize his need to face it, and to act."[3] After throwing down the gauntlet of individual and institutional responsibility to white leaders, he declared that "The level of effort—financial and political and personal—which is here required is fully comparable to the effort we now make as a nation in Vietnam."[4] By the end of 1967, his thinking had further crystallized, and in the *Ford Foundation Annual Report* for that year, he announced, "The first conclusion I offer is that the most deep-seated and destructive of all the causes of the Negro problem is still the prejudice of the white man. It is the white man's fears and hates that must have first place in explaining the condition of the American Negro."[5]

By 1969, the year the foundation funded the first round of grants to Black Studies programs, it was clear that Bundy's beliefs in fostering a "wider," "stronger," "deeper" effort on the part of whites to acknowledge America's race problem would be tied to his desire to institutionalize African American Studies within the academy. Indeed, implementing Black Studies became the primary method through which Bundy and the Ford Foundation would attempt to address the "Negro Problem," and they quickly set about the task of convincing administrators in colleges and universities that the new field was a tool for achieving democratic racial reform.[6] It was an intervention that would produce mixed results, but in many ways it was just what college administrators thought was needed as a balm to soothe racial tensions. Bundy and the program's officers at Ford hoped their strategy would also help the country at large.

As colleges and universities rushed to approve Black Studies, the reality of what such a field would mean for institutions, professors, students, and community became a topic of heated and often troubling debate. Nowhere was that debate more intense than among Black scholars. Significantly, the intellectual and practical struggle over how the new field would be implemented, framed, financed, and institutionalized often pit luminaries from the civil rights movement against those in the newly burgeoning Black Power movement. This confrontation both reflected and highlighted the strains between those who advocated racial integration as the solution to African American disenfranchisement and exclusion, and those who advocated a strategy of more aggressive militancy. Although the tone of the debate ranged from conciliatory to hostile, both groups searched for racial justice and equality, within higher education and outside of it. And the staging ground for their confrontation was centered on and within America's colleges and universities. The immediate issue may have been the best, most productive way for Black Studies to enter higher education, but the larger context was the question of whether racial integration or Black separatism was the best strategy for achieving racial equality. There was little middle ground.

Integrationists advocated reforming America through a strategy of racial diversification in institutions of higher learning —diversification not only in student bodies and faculties, but also in the curriculum. They argued that there were gaps and deficiencies within the curriculum that made it possible to ignore the important role Black people had played in the world, and that the racial bias inherent in the syllabi of most college courses could only be described as having a "white filter." Those who were most concerned about the content of college courses believed that the distortion had to be corrected so that all students —white and Black—could develop a more balanced perspective of history and contemporary issues. Black nationalists agreed about the deficiencies, but they also believed that "white education" had systematically and intentionally instilled a sense of racial inferiority in Black students. In order to shed that sense of inferiority and find a healthy identity, such students needed special courses on the "Black experience" taught by Black professors within the context of all-Black student centers, departments, and programs—and in some instances even colleges— established for this purpose on white college campuses.[7]

The contention was less about what the university owed its students of African descent than about the way the new field would impact the overall direction of the struggle for Black Power, Black rights (civil, economic, and intellectual), and the national acceptance of American citizens of African descent. The stakes were high indeed.

This is the context within which the Ford Foundation entered the debate. Headed by Bundy, a prominent member of the elite Eastern establishment, the Foundation inserted itself into the dispute and fashioned an institutional approach to issues of race, education, and American society that would come to shape the educational implementation of Black Studies for years to come. "The idea is to do things society is going to want after it has them," Bundy believed, declaring that he and the foundation "were eager for new ideas," and interested in moving "into hot firing lines."[8] While he and Ford initially considered a strategy of militant Black Power that advocated separatism as a political tool to solve America's racial problems, by the time Bundy began to approve the first round of grants in Black Studies in 1969, he had begun to embrace racial integration and diversity, both at the curricular and faculty level, as the most relevant concern for Black Studies. In either case, he believed that Black Studies was a necessary step toward solving America's problem with race or, as he termed it, the "Negro problem."[9] Although a number of competing models and ways of conceiving of and implementing Black studies would arise during the early 1970s, the model most replicated from one institution to the next, and the model most often emulated today, was crafted in the late 1960s and funded by the Ford Foundation at the behest of McGeorge Bundy.

Significantly, just as the war in Vietnam was often described as an effort to advance the cause of democracy around the world, a similar concern was at the heart of Bundy's embrace of Black Studies as a field. Given the cultural context of the period, and the various struggles over what Black Studies would mean, discussions about if and how it would enter the academy elicited the same types of emotions as those associated with the Vietnam War. Moreover, it was far from certain that Black Studies as a discipline would ever see the light of day, much less thrive, given the resistance of Black leaders associated with the civil rights movement, who viewed Black Studies as a form of segregation, and the reluctance of white college presidents and administrators, who felt that they were being strong-armed into embracing a field that they did not understand. As a result, the terrain that had to be traversed, as Black Studies took its first halting steps toward institutionalization, was rocky indeed.

RACE, REBELLION, AND BLACK STUDIES

As is clear from the previous chapter, the creation of the first African American Studies program was so closely tied to Black and white student activism that it is difficult to separate the institutionalization of the field from the upheaval, violence, and disruption so very common during the years it was conceived. The media images and the public's experiences of student unrest, Black Power, and campus violence seemingly characterized the sum total of what Black Studies was about. The protests at San Francisco State and Cornell University would define the field in the minds of many for decades to come. However, if the founding of African American studies was in part a strategy to restore peace to troubled college campuses, to respond to multiracial radical student groups demanding a more inclusive education, how then does one explain the appearance of such programs on so many campuses that were not experiencing upheaval and unrest? It is in answer to this question that the significance of McGeorge Bundy and the Ford Foundation looms large. Together, they crafted a meaning and understanding of Black Studies that made hesitant administrators see Black radicalism as part of the American mainstream and Black Studies as a step toward racial inclusion in America in general, and within higher education in particular. The strategy crafted by McGeorge Bundy and the Ford Foundation appealed to campus administrators, who believed it offered a solution to the problems of campus unrest, and to years of ignoring African American communities. However, at various points the foundation's strategy differed dramatically from the hopes of African Americans themselves.

While San Francisco State's department of African American Studies was the first in the country, in the next five years, by some counts, almost five hundred such programs were instituted on college campuses, and the number rises to over a thousand if one takes into account those programs started in junior colleges and high schools around the country.[10] Certainly Black protest and the threat of violence are one answer to the question of why Black Studies became so widespread a field. Indeed, Fabio Rojas, a sociologist interested in Ford's early involvement with Black Studies, has compiled and analyzed data on what he terms "black protest events," and concluded that the "peak of black insurgency coincides with the peak in the number of Black Studies program creations—1969."[11] As a result, it is certainly possible to say, given the period of unrest and dissatisfaction operating in the country, that many administrations wanted to ensure that their colleges did not fall prey to the political demands of radical students, as they had seen happen at San Francisco State and Cornell University. For them, the creation of Black Studies was a defensive move designed to forestall such trouble.

The fact that many administrators viewed Black Studies as insurance against student unrest was not lost on Ford Foundation officers, as they struggled to define for themselves a rationale for Black Studies that would achieve their particular aims. Early in 1969, in a memo to Bundy about the type of Black Studies programs they should support, one officer declared that a common result of student protest in relation to Black Studies was "Hastily conceived and academically unsound courses designed to stave off disaster rather than remedy curriculum deficiencies. In many of these cases, the students have not been clear in their own minds about what they wanted, other than more 'soul' in the curriculum, and the administration has often been willing to settle for a pacifier."[12] In short, such programs were often seen as cobbled-together offerings or band-aids, offered by college administrators to patch over the problem of past abuses, for the express purpose of avoiding African American student unrest and violence.

However, African American scholars and academics had different priorities for Black Studies on college campuses. For them, Black Studies quite simply represented a step toward the fulfillment of American ideals of democracy. From their viewpoint, if the battle for Black Studies and all that it was believed to symbolize had in fact been won, the question then became: What would the first programs look like? Who would teach in them, and what type of curriculum would best speak to the aims and interests of the radical, multiracial groups of students who had risked so much to gain a foothold for the new field in the academy?

STRUCTURED EQUALITY: METHODOLOGIES
OF BLACKNESS IN THE EARLY YEARS

Black Studies was viewed by Black students and community members with near-giddy anticipation in the first few months after its founding. Ironically, however, within African American political and intellectual communities, the field faced an immediate assault on its legitimacy, and there was considerable skepticism as to the ability of a new interdisciplinary department or field to provide students with useful information. Indeed, many wondered why a separate department was needed to house work by and about Black people; potentially, such an undertaking could further marginalize Black people in American society.

There was, however, another position on the question. As Nathaniel Norment has pointed out, by and large there were two divergent political-ideological perspectives on Black Studies in the first few years of its implementation. One was politically moderate and composed of African American intellectuals trained in traditional academic departments such as history, English, and sociology; the other was composed of those radicalized during the period and claiming Black nationalism as their guiding principle. In general, the moderate perspective asserted that African American Studies should be relevant to both African Americans and the university, providing a distinctive and rigorous education that would prepare students to become productive members of society. It was to be utilitarian in nature. They did not, however, believe that it was possible for the field to produce scholarship of high quality, or lead to the production of new forms of knowledge. They certainly did not believe that it was in any way connected with freedom.[13]

In addition to those willing to entertain the idea of some form of Black Studies, there were numerous Black scholars and political activists with long histories of fighting for racial inclusion and justice who vehemently opposed the new field. They were convinced that the still tenuous goal of integration would be undermined by the racial separatism at the heart of many Black Studies programs. Dr. Kenneth Clark was among those who objected to the separatism he believed to be inherent in the idea of Black Studies, and in 1969, upon hearing that Antioch College had agreed to begin a Black Studies program, he resigned from its board of directors. For him, merely instituting Black Studies because students asked for it was unconscionable. Clark was a highly respected social scientist who first came to national prominence in 1954 when he, along with his wife Mamie, conducted the now famous "doll study" that influenced the U.S. Supreme Court in the *Brown v. Topeka Board of Education* decision. That decision held that the doctrine of separate but equal was harmful to the psyches of African American children and relied on the findings of Clark and his wife, who had proven to the court's satisfaction that legal segregation harmed Black people by instilling a sense of inferiority. The court agreed that Clark's study, along with other compelling testimony, proved that legal separation between the races would have to be overturned.

In citing his reasons for stepping down from Antioch's board of directors, Clark chastised the college's administrators for couching their decision to institute Black Studies as support for the goals of racial integration and harmony. For him, "To encourage or endorse a separate Black program not academically equivalent to the college curriculum in general is to reinforce the Negro's inability to compete with whites for real power in the real society." After going on record with his skepticism regarding the relationship between narratives of Black Power and what he termed "real power," he concluded by noting, "It is no excuse to justify the deed by citing the demand."[14] Moreover, Clark believed that Black Studies was a short road to reinstituting the educational segregation of the races that he had helped to overturn almost fifteen years before.

Other notables joined Dr. Clark in his ambivalence about

Black Studies. For example, Bayard Rustin, an African American intellectual and civil rights activist, broadly supported the concept of Black Studies. However, he believed that the new field should be defined in the context of curricular diversity, whereby the history and culture of African Americans would be integrated into the larger curriculum of the university, rather than housed in a separate unit on college campuses. He argued that the study of Black people should be part of every college syllabus, and he was concerned that instituting a separate field of study could only lead to marginality. In addition, he thought that the field was implicated in ideological indoctrination and urged that the proponents of Black Studies cease to embrace the political rhetoric of upheaval and social action in which it was engaged. Rustin asked:

> Is black studies an educational program or a forum for ideological indoctrination? Is it designed to train qualified scholars in a significant field of intellectual inquiry, or is it hoped that its graduates will form political cadres prepared to organize the impoverished residents of the black ghetto? Is it a means to achieve psychological identity and strength, or is it intended to provide a false and sheltered sense of security, the fragility of which would be revealed by even the slightest exposure to reality? And finally, does it offer the possibility for better racial understanding, or is it a regression to racial separatism?[15]

No stranger to agitating for racial inclusion and struggling for African American equality, Rustin was a master strategist best remembered as a personal and intellectual mentor to Dr. Martin Luther King Jr. and as the lead organizer of the 1963 March on Washington, where King gave his famous "I Have a Dream" speech. Despite Rustin's long history with social justice movements and negotiation of racial acceptance for African

Americans, the relationship between Black Studies and Black Power proved difficult for him to accept. This was exacerbated by his belief that "The power—also the danger of 'black studies' as a slogan is that it can mean any or all of these things to different people."[16]

In addition to Clark and Rustin, another powerful African American leader, A. Philip Randolph, also publicly opposed what he assumed to be the mission and aims of Black Studies. In 1969, Randolph went so far as to edit and publish *Black Studies: Myths & Realities,* a book of essays and articles critical of the new field, suspicious of the motives of the whites who dared to support it, and also harshly critical of Black people who might want to do so. Much like Rustin and Clark, Randolph also had a long and sterling history of political activism. In 1925 he founded the Brotherhood of Sleeping Car Porters, at a time when half the affiliates of the American Federation of Labor (AFL) barred Black workers from membership. Despite fierce opposition, he built the first successful Black trade union. In addition, Randolph was responsible for President Franklin D. Roosevelt's actions to end employment discrimination against Blacks in the federal government and in industries with federal contracts. He warned Roosevelt that he would lead thousands in a protest march on Washington, D.C., if the president did not address this inequity. On June 25, 1941, Roosevelt issued Executive Order 8802, barring discrimination in defense industries and federal bureaus, and creating the Fair Employment Practices Committee. After World War II, Randolph founded the League for Nonviolent Civil Disobedience Against Military Segregation, resulting in Executive Order 9981, banning segregation in the armed forces, issued by President Harry S. Truman on July 26, 1948.

Thus, as a group, many of the heroes of a race-based civil rights movement, spanning a half-century, opposed the formation of Black Studies as an independent field of study. They were joined in some of their concerns by African American professors who supported Black Studies—with reservations. Some scholars, such as Martin Kilson, supported the moderate approach to Black Studies, but argued that it was not possible for an interdisciplinary new field to evolve into a scholarly and intellectually viable field without the curricular control of an established discipline.[17] By and large, those who opposed it, in whole or in part, refused to accept that Black Studies should be an intellectually separate, autonomous field of study, believing that such an endeavor was far too similar to instituting a racially segregated space within the academy that so many of them had fought against in public life. Black Studies, they feared, if based on separatism, could ultimately come to be viewed as an unequal and inferior part of the academy.

Given the esteem in which its critics were held, and the cogent and politically important nature of their concerns, what could those in support of founding the field as a segregated racial space possibly say in response? Without a basis in the traditional disciplines, what was to be the content of many of the early programs, and what could their existence mean in terms of larger questions concerning race, democracy, and citizenship? How would the new field add to, challenge, and/or mirror the production of knowledge as it had come to be understood in the academy? Questions such as these came to consume much of the discussion around Black Studies during the first few years of its founding.

Advocates believed that Black Studies should challenge the status quo in higher education, and they argued for a pedagogical approach that linked theory and practice, in order to alleviate the social problems within Black communities. Manning Marable, the founder and former chair of Columbia University's Institute for Research in African American Studies, has summed up this strain of thought as a belief that "black studies must also be an oppositional critique of the existing power arrangements and relations that are responsible for the systemic exploitation of black people."[18] Black sociologist St. Clair Drake would go further. In a lecture at Brooklyn College in September of 1969, he argued that the very term that most of the programs would choose to use, Black Studies, was in and of itself an indictment of American and Western European scholarship, because what had been called "objective intellectual activities were actually white studies in perspective and content." He went on to add that a "corrective bias, a shift in emphasis, is needed ... the present body of knowledge has an ideological element in it, and a counterideology is needed. Black Studies supply that counterideology."[19]

A few years later, another Black scholar would add a different dimension to the debate. Dr. Arthur L. Smith (who would change his name a few years later to Molefi Asante and go on to become a leading figure in the Afrocentrist branch of Black Studies) was the director of Afro American Studies and an Associate Professor of Speech Communication at UCLA in 1973. In a position paper, he offered another take on the methodology and utility of Black Studies, one that centered on Africa specifically and the relationship of an African past to modes of study appropriate for looking at contemporary African Americans. Terming his perspective, "Afrology," he suggested that Black Studies was the crystallization of the notions and methods of Black social scientists and humanists. What they explained, analyzed, and promulgated in papers, lectures, and private conversations had, he argued, taken shape as a new, creative discipline squarely resting on the foundations of an African past. He concluded by saying that "Afrology, that is Black Studies, is a singular academic achievement. It has made possible the conceptualization of Black perspectives and attitudes, thereby suggesting a new methodology."[20] For Smith, Black Studies had been instituted by Black people and was for Black people.

Within the context of higher education, those who advocated

organizing Black Studies so as to diversify the students, teachers, and curriculum on white college campuses strenuously opposed any suggestion that such programs should be aimed only at Black students. To allow such separatism, many argued, was to institute a new, Black-initiated form of segregation, and such an undertaking would undermine the basic tenets of racial inclusion so much at the heart of the civil rights movement. Indeed, given the very recent passage of the Voting Rights Amendment in 1965 and the fair housing laws of 1968, how, civil rights luminaries asked, could African Americans consider supporting an academic field organized in such as way as to point to racial difference and foster racial segregation on white college campuses? Theirs was a compelling argument.

But there was another one and, for many, equally compelling: Black Studies could and should be used to forge a new cultural awareness among African Americans that would move the social debate away from outmoded concepts emphasizing integration and assimilation and toward a model that offered Black self-knowledge and awareness as a basis for freedom. Advocates of this model acknowledged that their interest lay more in social revolution than in traditional forms of academic knowledge, and that they believed traditional institutional models were useless, oppressive, and irrelevant to and for Black students and the Black community. No, they insisted, Black Studies programs should seek to transform society by liberating the minds of African Americans and other oppressed people. Whites, they believed, could take care of themselves. Such programs must be committed to social action through close links with the off-campus Black community, and it was quite possible, at least initially, that this type of action, discussion, and education might need to take place in spaces that were limited to Black people only. For both groups, there were overarching principles at stake, and the terms of the institutionalization of African American Studies spoke to larger concerns of social justice, racial integration, and indeed fundamental questions about the nature of freedom.[21] Thus, McGeorge Bundy's and the Ford Foundation's interest in supporting Black Studies programs placed them in the midst of a very complex and heated debate within the larger Black community.

THE FORD FOUNDATION AND BLACK STUDIES: THE YALE CONFERENCE

One event functions as ground zero for the Ford Foundation's commitment to initiating Black Studies as a step toward finally and fully addressing the "Negro Problem" in America. The beginning of the public association between the Foundation and African American Studies came at the behest of Bundy in 1968. That year, in a speech at Yale University, the former dean of Harvard University began to shape the feel, focus, and future of African American Studies as it entered the academic universe. The topic of the conference was Black Studies, and those who participated were called together to support the position of that university's Black Student Alliance, in its call for "including the study of Afro-American societies and cultures in the curriculum of Yale College."[22] Having already spent the better part of a year trying to convince campus administrators that their concerns were valid and that a degree-granting program was viable, important, and intellectually defensible, the students chose to sponsor a gathering that was billed as "an educational experience for professional educators."[23]

Such a gathering was unprecedented, even in the spring of 1968, against the backdrop of increasingly strident demands. Also unprecedented was the range of scholars and academics who assembled. The speakers were white and African American male scholars and academics and constituted a broad range of disciplines, interests, and methodological persuasions. Those who called for African American Studies to base its intellectual underpinnings on various strains of Black nationalism, as well as what would come to be known as Afrocentricity, spoke to proponents of Black Studies models that were integrationist in nature and to others who were openly hostile to the intellectual validity of such an undertaking. Some, like Harold Cruse, the author of the highly influential *Crisis of the Negro Intellectual,* published in 1967, argued that "How best to respond to demands for black studies is a very complicated problem because we have two distinct trends in the Black movement."[24] After describing one strain as a radical or revolutionary thrust, and the other as the slow reformist impulse, he went on to suggest that "Black cultural nationalism has to be seen as an attempt, a necessarily historical attempt, to deal with another kind of cultural nationalism that is implied in our society, namely, the cultural nationalism of the dominant white group."[25]

Cruse was followed by Martin Kilson, a tenured professor in Harvard's Department of Government. Kilson argued that "The best approach in addressing this topic is to assess conceptually what the black experience has been and has meant. Such assessment, I think, is not easy at all. For one thing, what contemporaneous yardstick does one use to define the historical limits, the starting point, and the context of the black experience?"[26] He concluded by saying, "I personally understand the viewpoint as held by black nationalists. Indeed, I am compassionate toward it. But my intellect rejects it."[27] Throughout the two-day conference, the speakers expounded on their beliefs about the reasons for the current absence of Black Studies in the curriculum, as well as ways in which its inclusion could most beneficially enhance the academy at large.

One of the last speakers was McGeorge Bundy. As a graduate of Yale, and having used the foundation's resources to underwrite the cost of the conference, he was in a powerful position to mediate between the various factions jockeying for position. He was one of the only speakers not holding an academic teaching position, one of only a few white men to address the gathering, and the only member of a philanthropic organization to either attend or speak. He began his remarks by telling those assembled that the past twenty-four hours had been "a great white experience" and recounting his affinity for the room in which they were gathered, as it had been the "scene of a series of examinations in German, French, and other low, white topics."[28]

While surely a reference to the overwhelming number of speakers who continually referenced "the black experience" in their various remarks and reflections, Bundy's references to the white experience could not have helped but surprise the participants. He moved immediately from those observations to revealing that the Course of Study Committee and the Yale College faculty had already decided to approve the students' request for a degree-granting program organized around the study of people of African descent—although a number of speakers following Bundy suggested that he was overly optimistic about the new program, especially given the fact that the committee had not even met, as far as the students knew. Nonetheless, Bundy would surprise quite a few participants by expressing his "strong agreement with the direction in which Professor Robert Dahl and his committee propose to move."[29] He then offered his own theory of how Black Studies could most helpfully and permanently enter the university.

His words would prove to be prophetic. In his first two years as the president of the Ford Foundation, he almost doubled the amount of money dispensed by the national affairs division. He spent almost forty million dollars during that twenty-four month period, much of it for programs aimed at addressing the race problem. His was a promise of help to come. Indeed, his grants to African American Studies programs totaled more than ten million dollars and supported two dozen programs between 1968 and 1972. As a result, Bundy was able to legitimize the study of people of African descent in the academy. At the same time, he set the terms of its entrance into those hallowed halls in ways that were often at variance with those called for by many of the African American speakers at the Yale conference. Specifically, Bundy would tell his listeners that it was clear that the time for African American Studies to be seen as a legitimate academic enterprise was long past due. He added, "the first part of the problem, is there a subject here? Really was settled before we came, and is doubly settled now."[30]

After affirming the academic value of Black Studies, Bundy turned to the heart of the matter for many of the previous speakers: whether the new field would enter the academy aligned with Black nationalist sentiment and responsive chiefly to the needs of an African American community and constituency. One of the speakers, Maulana Karenga, had earlier stated that there were a number of things Yale needed to do as it moved toward instituting African American Studies: "First, nonintervention with regard to the Black community: stop imposing yourself through projects that only benefit you and the white community, or business community. Stop trying to make political decisions about what we do. Do not pass value judgments on what we do."[31] Overall, Karenga argued for the political relevance of the newly forming field of African American Studies, and for its ownership by African Americans outside of the university as well as within it.

In his remarks, Bundy addressed Karenga directly: "It was made very clear by Maulana Karenga that his interest in these matters is a political interest, and that his purpose is to establish a balance of power. That seems to me a first-class purpose and a proper target. It also seems to me not to be the way to define the interesting topics in Black history."[32] Bundy suggested that the strength of Black Studies was not in its politics, identity, or nationalistic sensibility, but rather in its ability to enter the academy and desegregate the faculty and curriculum of traditionally "white" disciplines such as art, history, literature, and sociology.

In many ways Bundy's life had prepared him well to take just such a stand. Indeed, if the issue involved power and its use in American culture, discussing how best to wield it meant that he was on solid ground. If nothing else, he had been reared to hold the reins of power and was certainly comfortable discoursing on the ways it could and should work.

Born in Boston to a family well established in the cultural, social, intellectual, and political elite of New England, McGeorge Bundy was related to prominent figures on both sides of his family. His father, Harvey Hollister Bundy, was a lawyer who served as secretary to Oliver Wendell Holmes, the assistant secretary of state from 1931 to 1933, and as special assistant to the secretary of war from 1941 to 1945. His mother, Katherine Lawrence Putnam Bundy, was the daughter of Harvard president A. Lawrence Lowell.

After attending the Groton School, Bundy studied mathematics at Yale, earning a B.A. with highest honors in 1940. The following year, he became a junior fellow of Harvard's Society of Fellows, turning his attention to the study of foreign relations. In 1942 Bundy left Harvard and served briefly in the Office of Facts and Figures under the noted Archibald MacLeish. He then joined the army, memorizing the eye chart to hide his nearsightedness. He rose from private to captain, serving on the staff that planned the invasions of Sicily and France. In 1946, Bundy returned to the Society of Fellows, collaborating with Henry L. Stimson, secretary of war under President Franklin Roosevelt, on Stimson's autobiography, *On Active Service in Peace and War* (1948). In 1949, McGeorge Bundy began teaching government and world affairs at Harvard. Although he held no doctorate in any field, he quickly received tenure, and by 1953, at the age of thirty-four, he was appointed dean of Harvard's Faculty of Arts and Sciences. Six years later, he was called to the Kennedy White House as the country's national security advisor.[33]

It is impossible to study the war in Vietnam without encountering McGeorge Bundy and his brother, William, who was the director of the CIA during the Johnson administration and deputy assistant secretary of defense under President Kennedy. The Bundy brothers were part of the intellectual establishment that, at least initially, relentlessly pursued that war. Indeed, the two were part of the group of Ivy League–educated, Skull and Bones membership, young white men who shaped and carried out America's foreign policy during the 1960s. Both were instrumental in managing the Bay of Pigs incident and what could easily be described as the most dangerous nuclear confrontation of the entire Cold War—the Cuban missile crisis.[34] Although he had clearly been exposed to and immersed in political power for a great deal of his life, it was his relationship with Black Power that would attract so much attention in his later years.

McGEORGE BUNDY AND BLACK POWER

Bundy clearly understood that the emergence of a Black Power movement represented a distinct shift in the Black political agenda, from civil rights to power. Essayist, playwright, and novelist James Baldwin offered an explanation for the thinking behind the Black Power movement in his 1963 collection of essays, *The Fire Next Time:* "The only thing white people have that black people need, or should want, is power—and no one holds power forever."[35] The shift in political rhetoric from rights to power signaled the end of many interracial alliances principally structured around gaining civil rights and freedom for African Americans. Indeed, Stokely Carmichael first used the Black Power slogan in June 1966, during a protest march in Mississippi, soon after his election as chairman of the interracial Student Nonviolent Coordinating Committee. Under his leadership, the organization would expel white students, as discussed in the previous chapter, but they would flourish in their own, the Students for a Democratic Society.

Similarly, the Black Panther Party, which was founded in Oakland in 1966, called on African Americans to embrace their identity and throw off the oppression of white supremacy and Black self-hatred. The party was deeply skeptical about the nonviolent ideology underpinning much of the thinking of the civil rights movement. In their call for armed defense and revolution, the Black Panthers reflected the voice of Black Caribbean psychologist Frantz Fanon, who had declared, "Violence is a cleansing force. It frees the native from his despair and inaction; it makes him fearless and restores his self-respect."[36] Although often defined by their willingness to use violence, the Panther Party's guiding document makes it clear that their version of Black Power was deeply influenced by the founding principles and documents central to the American experience of freedom and liberation. The ten-point platform of the Black Panther Party began with the words: "We want freedom. We want power to determine the destiny of our Black Community."[37] Perhaps it was his reflection on this and similar statements that led Bundy to write in the Ford Foundation's 1967 *Ford Foundation Annual Report* about the forthcoming financial support for "legitimately militant black leaders...and their properly angry words." He added, "Who can deny the right of young black students to have a part of their lives kept black? And who can be surprised that many of them exercise that right?"[38] Whether he was influenced by a specific text or not, however, Bundy could not have helped being immersed in representations and images associated with Black Power. By the late 1960s, they were ubiquitous.

Indeed, by then the spectacle of Black Power was beginning to become a commodity. Long before the ink was dry on the contract between student groups and college administrators at San Francisco State and Cornell University, and certainly before the elation of victory had fully subsided and the congratulatory parties had ended, the topics of Black Studies, Black Power, and

student protest had become popular in the worlds of mainstream publishing and film. While colleges and universities were
being called to task for offering an "irrelevant" education in the
torrid political period of the 1960s, the visual images of urban
African Americans willing to embrace violence and the rhetoric
of Black Power were going mainstream—especially after the ex-
plosions at San Francisco State and Cornell University. Between
1968 and 1971, the book titles came fast and furiously: *Black
Studies: Threat-or-Challenge; Black Power U.S.A.; White Reflections on Black Power; Dialectics on Black Power; Whither
Black Power; Black Power and Urban Unrest; Black Power
and Student Rebellion; Black Power and the American Myth;
New Perspectives on Black Studies; The Black Revolt: The Civil
Rights Movement, Ghetto Uprisings, and Separatism; Profiles in
Black Studies,* and *A Black Nun Looks at Black Power* were just
a few of the hundreds of titles that attempted to explain—or to
understand—the relationship between student activism, Black
Power, and the new field of Black Studies.

At the same time, a genre of film termed "blaxploitation"
capitalized on the rhetoric and rationale of Black Power and
Black Studies. In 1971, Melvin Van Peebles produced *Sweet
Sweetback's Baadasssss Song,* the story of a Black man who
struck back at white police officers who attempted to brutalize
him while he was in police custody. That film would be followed
the same year by Gordon Parks's *Shaft,* the story of another
Black man who did battle with the corrupt forces of white
power in New York, in order to exonerate a wrongly accused
Black man. Both became hugely successful box-office hits.

In the atmosphere created by the news footage of Black Panthers taking over the California state capitol armed with legally
obtained and permissible guns and rifles, and the 1970 spectacle
of Angela Davis's photograph on the FBI's Ten Most Wanted
list, at times it must have felt to those shaping the new field
as if all eyes were on them. Their deliberations took place in an

atmosphere that was only a little less public than the world of book publishers and readers, viewers of the nightly news, or movie theaters featuring the newest Black Power superhero. While in 1966 Bundy would claim not to understand it, two years later he not only had had some experience with Black Power activism, but he had funded organizations that advocated it. Given the fallout from his actions, by 1969, he had rejected any form of Black Power as an organizing principle for African American Studies.

During 1967 and 1968, the years preceding the Yale conference, Bundy used resources from the Ford Foundation to support a number of key, highly visible political contests and social strategies undertaken by Black Power proponents. Given that the shift in the struggle for Black rights had by the mid-1960s moved from South to North, with an attendant shift in focus from legal to economic issues, the Ford Foundation began to look for ways to fund groups in urban areas interested in addressing the economic inequity experienced by African Americans. In a sense, this was an understandable shift that extended and followed up on initiatives already put forward in the foundation's Gray Areas program, which was functioning in six inner cities in the early 1960s.[39] Among other things, the Gray Areas program was designed to provide funds to teach those caught in difficult economic circumstances to organize politically. On the eve of a mayoral election in Cleveland, one such grant was made to the Cleveland chapter of the Congress On Racial Equality (CORE), then under the direction of Floyd McKissick. The Ford Foundation gave the organization $175,000, half for voter registration, and half to train community workers, who were then to help other African Americans become more politically astute.

Carl A. Stokes was elected as the first African American mayor of a major American city. However, many believed that Ford had stepped out of line by funding CORE, an organization deemed to be militant by many in the political mainstream, although that was not its early history. It began as an integrated organization that opposed segregation through nonviolent social strategies. However, by 1967 the organization's president would explicitly repudiate the phrase "civil rights," delete the word "multiracial" from its constitution, and adopt the more militant stance of Black Power. In a sense, CORE's political trajectory exemplified the changing climate, and illustrates how the rhetoric of Black Power came to take a primary position within the Ford Foundation's thinking about the best ways to address racial issues in America. For many of the same reasons that CORE evolved from an integrationist organization to one advocating Black Power, Black revolution, and insurgency, Bundy believed that to be effective, "one had to reach Black people where they lived. It made no sense to him for the organization to fund reasonable-sounding integrationists if they had no following in urban areas."[40] He, like CORE, understood that one had to "speak the language" of the Black urban poor and accept their world-view and even, perhaps, deal with their real anger."[41] One Ford Foundation officer explained that the grant would show that "a militant organization can work within the system."[42]

By 1963 CORE had already shifted attention to segregation in the North and West, where two-thirds of the organization's chapters were located. As CORE undertook to build its credibility as a Black protest organization, membership in these Northern chapters became almost entirely Black, and CORE's multiracial ideology and commitment to nonviolent protest strategies were increasingly challenged by its changing membership. At the same time that tactics were being questioned, so was the leadership. In 1966, under mounting pressure and with the organization losing members, influence, and financial support, James Farmer stepped down as national director and was replaced by the more militant Floyd McKissick, who endorsed the term "Black Power" and the separatist strategy and rhetoric that went with it. One year later, the Ford Foundation gave the organization the $175,000 grant, as a part of their effort to provide continuing support for what they then saw as a Northern manifestation of the primarily Southern-based civil rights movement.

Although Bundy was firm in his commitment to giving the organization the money, he was aware that his actions might raise a few eyebrows. Bundy explained at a press conference that his board had considered the grant "with particular care." Indeed, "of the 16 Trustees, only Henry Ford himself expressed any apprehension."[43] Bundy went on to say that "neither Mr. McKissick nor I suppose that this grant requires the two of us, or our organizations to agree on all public questions."[44] He was giving the money to CORE in the hopes that they would use it to help channel the Black rage erupting as rebellions all over the country into a more constructive way of registering grievances. The impact of the grant on the mayoral election was the first sign to Bundy and the foundation of the trouble that embracing Black power as a political strategy could bring. The fallout undoubtedly influenced his thinking about Black Power as he reflected on funding Black Studies programs a year later.

CLEVELAND: BACKGROUND OF AN ELECTION

In the years leading up to 1967, the year Carl A. Stokes was mayor, Cleveland, like many cities with large urban populations, was making some effort to address its serious, longstanding, and festering racial problems. Indeed, the city held a series of public hearings in April of 1966 that documented the extent of the economic disparity between Black and white Clevelanders. The hearings revealed that the median income for African Americans was $3,966, as opposed to $5,200 for whites. While 9 percent of all African Americans, male and female, were unemployed, the unemployment figures for white communities hovered around 2.3 percent—and almost 58 percent of African American men under the age of twenty-five were unemployed.[45] This was just the type of economic inequity that Black Power proponents were attempting to address, and that the Ford Foundation felt bound to alleviate, as a means of addressing the "Negro Problem." Lack of economic opportunity had inflamed the cities, several of which had already erupted into fiery and violent riots.

Once news of the differences in economic opportunity was reported, violence erupted that would take four lives. Black pain, rage, and despair bubbled to the surface, and in the midst of the urban uprising, instances of police brutality further exacerbated the racial situation. Symbolizing police contempt, Police Chief Richard Wagner "rode into the midst of the rioting neighborhoods during the riots armed with his personal hunting rifle, which he used against snipers."[46] When a woman, searching for her children, was killed by gunfire, Wagner remarked, "There was a similar occurrence in the Chicago riots. They sacrifice one person and blame it on police brutality."[47] In short, unresolved issues of economic disparity, Black anger, and police brutality were shrouded in the background of an election that would be a momentous event in terms of race. The stage was set in Cleveland for a national test to divert Black anger into Black Power and for the whole to be channeled into conventional politics.[48]

Cleveland's political leadership was caught in the surge of a dramatic change in political strategy and ideology. Mayor Locher was unfortunate to be in office when the "civil rights movement merged with the rhetoric of black power and the whole crested in anger."[49] Although he and other business leaders had long had working relationships with established leaders in the Black community, they had little, if any, understanding of how to talk to the new leaders who were emerging and beginning to impact corporate America's business of making money. Bundy and others understood that riots and racial issues directly affected the business community, and a year earlier they had sought to discuss the reasons for corporate America to support the interests of Black leaders who supported Black Power. Mc-George Bundy told listeners in a speech in 1966 that "Something would have to be done about the urban problem." If Blacks burned American cities, "The white man's companies will have to take the losses."[50] Upon hearing his comments, Black scholar Robert Allen, in *Black Awakening in Capitalist America,* quoted Bundy and added, "White America is not so stupid as not to comprehend that elemental fact. Thus, the Ford Foundation was on its way to becoming the most important though least publicized organization manipulating the militant black movement."[51]

In Cleveland, the business community in the late 1950s had pushed City Hall into massive urban renewal projects that were designed to revitalize a once vibrant Cleveland. The renewal efforts triggered the mass evictions of people, primarily Black and poor, from the central areas of the city into the urban area known as Hough. Poor whites then moved out en masse, leaving a ghetto of housing already substandard and densely populated. School desegregation was another highly charged racial issue in Cleveland, as well as in other Northern cities. The death of the Reverend Bruce Klunder, run over by a bulldozer at a site where there was a protest, added to community passions. Riots, the dislocation of poor African Americans, segregated school districts, and the violent death of a beloved social activist soon made clear that something would have to change. Carl Stokes decided to run for mayor.[52]

Stokes took stock of the growing turmoil and was able to use it to his advantage. He later wrote in his autobiography, *Promises of Power:* "In the spring and summer of 1967 when the power structure was grooming me as the man to back in the mayor's race, I was invited to the most exclusive clubs in Cleveland to talk to them about myself and what I hoped to do for Cleveland."[53] Although he was apparently being groomed for leadership, the popular belief at the time was that the city's demographics would give any white candidate an easy win over a Black candidate. However, no one was prepared for the infusion of resources for voter registration that would ultimately lead to Stokes's victory. This is where the Ford Foundation stepped in with the grant to help CORE to organize and register Black voters.

Ford's direct grant to CORE was not its only grant to the Cleveland registration efforts. An October 1967 memorandum from Martin Luther King's Southern Christian Leadership Conference revealed that $27,899 given by Ford to SCLC was used in Cleveland to aid in registering voters, with the hope of electing Stokes mayor. SCLC had received a $230,000 grant from the Ford Foundation that year. While Bundy would later argue that they were doing no more than performing a public service for poor African Americans, it looked to many white observers as if the foundation had intervened in the political process on the side of a particular candidate. The *Boston Globe* would editorialize, "If one foundation can help elect a good mayor, why cannot another elect a bad one?"[54] By 1969, President Nixon told one of his aides to ask the Internal Revenue Service to look at the "activities of left-wing organizations which are operating with tax-exempt funds." The aide responded that "Certainly we ought to act in time to keep the Ford Foundation from again financing Carl Stokes' mayoralty campaign in Cleveland." Nixon directed the aide to "follow up hard on this."[55] In addition to attracting the attention of the president, the foundation's actions alarmed both Stokes's opponents and several U.S. congressmen, and hearings were held to look into the role the Ford Foundation had played in the election.

The other half of the grant to CORE, earmarked for the training of community organizers and workers, also grew controversial, and it too hinted at the possible perils of supporting Black self-determination and power. Several dozen youths were paid $1.50 an hour to attend classes at CORE's headquarters.

These courses focused on Black history and heritage, but also on what one CORE official called "the decision on revolution or not."[56] A Black city councilman who opposed the program said the youngsters were being taught "race hatred" and that he had heard one telling a group of younger children that "we are going to get guns and take over."[57] To calls to cease the funding of CORE and any like organizations, Bundy replied, "I see it as a flowering of what Black Power could be." He added, "Motherhood, boy scouts, voter registration. Everyone's for it as an alternative to rocks and fire bombs. And it turned out that way in Cleveland." Despite the turmoil, the funding for CORE was renewed for another year.[58]

The resulting media and political firestorm may be the reason McGeorge Bundy was much more cautious about Black Power strategies by 1969, when he would commit the Ford Foundation to a far less controversial approach to Black Studies, as it first entered the academic universe. In addition, while the Cleveland election was clearly one link in a larger chain of addressing the "Negro Problem" through support of Black Power, another event in 1968 would prove politically costly to both McGeorge Bundy personally and the Ford Foundation as an organization. The event that Jerald E. Podair pinpoints as "the end of illusions for both New York City and America," the 1968 teacher strikes in Ocean Hill-Brownsville, an area of Brooklyn, marked the beginning of decades of racial conflict in New York City. Coming hot on the heels of the Stokes election, the strikes undoubtedly helped to influence Ford's growing caution toward Black Power and ultimately Black Studies.[59]

In 1968, the schools of Ocean Hill-Brownsville became part of an "experiment," funded by the Ford Foundation, which gave community control to just a few of the poorest school districts in the city. It was a decision they would arguably come to regret.[60]

OCEAN HILL-BROWNSVILLE

The plan to allow community control of the schools was an experiment Bundy was willing to undertake. Given the fact that many white parents were violently opposed to any form of integration in the schools (this held true for a majority of parents in the outer boroughs of New York—Queens, Staten Island, the Bronx, and Brooklyn), Bundy came to believe that it was a waste of time and needlessly divisive to continue with efforts to integrate. The education of the children should come first. In keeping with his embrace of Black Power, and with Black community control still working itself out in Cleveland, he decided to experiment with "a little Black Power in the classroom." Indeed, Bundy believed that Black Power might make "the schools more responsive and more relevant to students and perhaps their reading and math scores would improve."[61] Instead, the result was a bitter teachers' strike.

The Ocean Hill-Brownsville teachers' strike of 1968 split New York City. Most Black New Yorkers "perceived community control of the schools in Black neighborhoods as part of the struggle for racial justice; they saw the teacher strike as a defense of white privilege. Most white New Yorkers perceived Black community control of the schools as a power grab; they saw the strike as a defense of a society based on individual achievement."[62] Within weeks of the foundation's $59,000 grant, the activists who made up the board found themselves at odds with some dozen allegedly "incompetent" teachers charged by the school board with being disloyal to the decentralization experiment. The board was largely Black, the teachers were white. In May 1968, the offending teachers were asked to leave their posts, and when the union came to their defense, the local board went to war against the union. They hired several hundred irregular teachers and began organizing people from the Black community to demonstrate at the schools. Once the dust had settled, "white middle-class protest stripped Black community control of its elite white support and assured its defeat."[63]

Throughout the fall of 1968, the Ocean Hill-Brownsville schools were the scene of daily violence, and the conflict in the district was the topic of national news reports. A typical day brought out pickets and counterpickets, shouting at each other across wooden police horses. At the same time, "both sides organized rallies at City Hall; both spread hateful and largely racial innuendo. Black anti-Semitism (many of the teachers were Jewish) vied in fury with whites' race-charged fear and anger, and the cumulative venom spiraled out of control."[64] The eight schools in the Ocean Hill-Brownsville district were at the center of the storm, and many white teachers there reported they feared for their lives. The striking union shut down the entire school system. More than one million students missed over a month of classes in the fall.

In the end, the conflict was settled when the state education authorities approved a less extreme version of Bundy's recommendations on community control. Nonetheless, Ford paid a high cost. Conservative journalists and congressmen seized on the foundation's involvement in both Ocean Hill and Cleveland. Taken together, the fallout from the Cleveland election and from the experiment with the schools in New York put Ford on notice as to what was at stake in its embrace of Black Power. As they moved to institutionalize Black Studies, they would not make that same mistake again. At the same time, in order to ensure that the foundation would tread more lightly in the future, Congress enacted a number of controls aimed at curtailing the power of all foundations, not just Ford.

In January of 1969, the House Ways and Means Committee began hearings on tax reform, and philanthropy was high on the list of topics to be addressed. In a speech before the committee on the opening day of hearings, the chairman asked, "Are the giant foundations on the road to becoming political machines? ... Does the Ford Foundation have a grandiose design to bring vast political, economic, and social changes to the nation in the 1970s? I need not tell you gentlemen what can happen in a local, state or national election where this kind of money is turned loose, directly or indirectly, in behalf of their favorite candidates."[65] Congress ended up passing an elaborate array of regulations on foundations. The federal oversight and questioning came on the eve of the Ford Foundation's meeting to approve the first grants to Black Studies programs and departments. Their attitude toward Black Power had by then changed significantly.

4

BLACK STUDIES IN WHITE AND BLACK

The Ford Foundation Funds Black Studies

Given the public outcry over Ford's involvement with Black Power, as the foundation prepared to award the first round of grants to Black Studies programs, it no longer wished to support or fund proposals that advocated any type of militancy. Accordingly, the relationship of money to power and power to race could not have been more different as Ford moved from one strategy to the next. During an earlier period, Bundy believed that Black Power was an understandable form of Black anger that Ford could support in the hopes of strengthening Black communities and helping them achieve racial parity. However, by 1969, he believed that Black Studies was a tool that could lead to heightened levels of racial understanding and acceptance on the part of whites. There was no longer any room in his thinking for Black separatism, anger, or militancy. While Ford's motivation for its union with Black Power advocates in 1968 was an attempt to build a new pathway leading directly to interracial cooperation, the outcome exposed the pitfalls of that approach. If some Black Studies proponents had the desire to transform American institutions of higher education, the Ford Foundation saw itself as transformative in another regard. The foundation's choices regarding the types of programs and institutional structures it would support had far-ranging consequences for the future of Black Studies, as well as for racial interaction on campuses.

From the late 1960s through 1970, Bundy and the foundation officers were cognizant of what was at stake and the complicated nature of the issue as they began to deliberate over the initial twelve grants to be funded. As they pored over the hundreds of applications submitted by schools, students, faculty, and administrators, they realized that they needed to catch up. The momentum around instituting Black Studies was progressing rapidly.

BLACK STUDIES GRANT MAKING AND THE FORD FOUNDATION

The growth in the field, from one department in 1968 to over five hundred by 1972, caught almost everyone by surprise. Black Studies programs, courses, and departments were popping up in colleges, high schools, and junior colleges all over the United States. While the students responsible for the strike that produced the first department of Black Studies at San Francisco State must have been proud to see where their efforts had led, the Ford Foundation was concerned by the unchecked rate of growth. Although they were not especially interested in slowing it down, they did want to shape the nature of the field. Indeed, Bundy and the handful of program officers responsible for making decisions about the first grants believed that—given Black Studies' need to negotiate its growing pains, and with such disparate forces pulling at it—the new field would ultimately disappoint and disillusion, if not properly guided. Should Black Studies fail to take hold at the outset, some at Ford were concerned that the window of opportunity would be gone.[1]

Toward that end, the grants made between 1968 and 1971, with two exceptions, were awarded to programs and institutions that viewed Black Studies as a means to diversify a predominantly white curriculum and institution, promote integration, and perhaps most importantly, give the more militant version of separatism and Black Nationalism a wide berth.

Given the fact that just a few short years before, Bundy had eloquently written that "The American Negro will have to have
much more economic and political power than he has today
before the rest of us have any reason to believe that he has more
than his fair share. Meanwhile, the Ford Foundation will work
with Negro leaders of good will and peaceful purpose without
any anguished measurement of their position on the issue of a
separated power of blackness as against the continuing claim to
integration."[2] It is notable that, by 1969, a significantly different
logic was operating in regard to the funding practices embraced
by Ford in relation to Black Studies. A proposal based on a "separated" Black power stood no chance of receiving funding.

Ironically, this vision of Black Studies held true whether the
program was instituted on a college campus that was predominantly Black or on one that was predominantly white. On Black
college campuses, funds were provided for projects to compile
and distribute teaching materials to white colleges interested in
desegregating their curricula but lacking the expertise on their
own faculties. The decision to structure Black Studies in a way
that not only sidestepped the demands of militant, nationalist,
or radical students but also made it intellectually and structurally dependent on traditional disciplines was one that many
program officers knew would raise eyebrows and perhaps blood
pressures. Indeed, on the eve of their final decisions, there was
discussion among officers about the political and racial makeup
of the external committee that would make final recommendations about the grants. One program officer, Roger Wilkins,
urged Bundy to fight "The temptation to pick only those voices
that will probably agree with us," and warned that "The tension
that comes from diversity ought to stretch to us."[3]

As a result, the process that Ford undertook to gain recommendations involved substantial discussion and input. Bundy
and the rest of the program officers understood, as Wilkins
wrote to Bundy, that "the whole issue of black studies is so

highly charged with emotion and so close to the hearts of black scholars and students that there clearly could be a number of deep, hidden potholes down the road." He counseled Bundy to create a "review committee which contains a number of distinguished black educators" in order to demonstrate the foundation's sensitivity to the perception that they were only interested in having "white people make all the decisions about things that are vital" to Black people. He strongly urged Bundy to "be sure that our advisory group includes not only representatives of the older and more settled elements of the academic community, but that it also include the views of the younger and angrier black scholars."[4]

However, when Ford consulted with professors and administrators about the ideological lens they should use to guide their deliberations, they tended to select scholars, both Black and white, who were in prestigious academic positions and saw Black Studies as an opportunity to further the goal of interdisciplinary study in the traditional disciplines. Further, these scholars were often hostile, or at the very least suspicious, toward the idea of Black Studies as a field if it was not promoted as a means to create greater racial awareness among whites. To structure Black Studies in such a way as to ensure its longevity and autonomy, or in a manner that allowed for an overemphasis on exploration of Black cultural identity and history was, as far as Ford was concerned, wrongheaded. As one of Ford's advisors succinctly stated, "Fads come and go."[5] For example, when the highly respected Black economist Sir Arthur Lewis, a professor of economics and international affairs at Princeton University's Woodrow Wilson School, evaluated a collection of grant proposals, he responded that it was wise to avoid making Black Studies its own field. He felt that potential Black Studies majors should stay within traditional disciplines, such as economics, English, history, or sociology and take Black Studies courses as electives. Lewis believed that Black students who were clamor-

ing to take courses in the field, and whites interested in supporting the field, first had to "distinguish between the history of
black people as a group or groups, and the achievements of individual blacks (X was the first American to do this or that).
Black militants want the latter, for its therapeutic value, to bol-
ster black pride." After assuring Bundy that the type of history Black militants advocated was "history as taught in grade
school" and as such far beneath consideration, Lewis then
turned his attention to the Black student demand for Black
teachers. Here as well, he cautioned Bundy, remarking that the
"student demand for black teachers is associated with the desire
for black studies to be taught inspirationally, and should therefore be rejected along with the inspirational approach." As an
alternative perspective, he pointed out that any program in
Black Studies could most productively be organized around its
utility for white students, saying, "Princeton's experience is that
there is an enormous demand for black studies among white students" and arguing that this perspective made the most sense
because "white students sharpen the discussion, since they are
not dominated by the black militants, who discourage awkward
questions and frank answers." He ended his recommendations about Black Studies by warning that the Ford Foundation
should proceed cautiously and think clearly about heeding his
suggestions, because "Colleges, which have hastily put on undergraduate inspirational courses will be caught with faculty,
programs and students who are generally despised, and black
studies will be just one more source of black shame and inferiority in such institutions."[6]

McGeorge Bundy made a point of writing back to Lewis to
inform him when they had finally approved the first batch of
grants and to acknowledge that the board of trustees had signed
off on them without a problem. Finally, Bundy told Lewis that
he would be surprised if there was any serious disagreement
within the foundation with the views he had put forth. Indeed,

far from provoking disagreement, Lewis's position in fact garnered substantial support, and as foundation officers began to review grant proposals, they used his perspective to either fund or deny applications.[7]

Once the foundation had identified the handful of programs that they wanted to fund, there was still discussion regarding how the foundation's efforts would be perceived. Accordingly, one of the program officers responsible for researching how Black Studies could most effectively be embarked upon stated that the foundation would have to act quickly if it wanted to impact the field. He noted that "The clock is ahead of the Foundation with respect to Afro-American studies. No one knows precisely how many colleges and universities are going to launch new courses or new programs of studies in the field come September, but a conservative estimate would place the number at several hundred."[8] While acknowledging that not much could be done to influence the direction of those programs already in the pipeline, the report does note that the Ford Foundation can "make an important contribution to the orderly development of this hitherto-neglected field of studies by helping a few strategic institutions get off on the right foot. The grants proposed here are designed to do that." Not content to concede that programs were developing without benefit of Ford Foundation guidance and support, the report makes clear that "on many campuses, courses in Afro-American studies will have to be established this September whether they are good, bad, or indifferent. There is, however, reason to expect that some of the courses developed under these grants may set some standards of quality by which other institutions can measure and eventually revise their own offerings."[9] Undoubtedly, the foundation was committed to guiding the shape of the field of Black Studies.

In examining the outcome of funding, the internal discussions at Ford made clear that, although they hoped to craft a particular understanding of what Black Studies could offer campuses in terms of racial relationships, they realized that such programs would not function as safety valves, capable of relieving all the social and racial tension building up in the country. They also knew, however, that many administrators and students believed that Black Studies programs would accomplish precisely that. In closing his ruminations about Black Studies, Roger Wilkens concluded by saying that he and the rest of the committee did "not believe that Afro-American studies programs will prove to be an unmitigated blessing to the students, faculty, or administrators at the institutions that embark upon them. They will not provide a 'cure' for campus unrest at white or black colleges, because the unrest goes much deeper than dissatisfaction with the curriculum, and even at their best they are not likely to completely satisfy the demands of their advocates."[10] It was then even more crucial to offer an organizing principle for Black Studies that Ford hoped would realistically address the racial crisis brewing in the country at large and on college campuses in particular.

James Armsey, in an interoffice memorandum written to McGeorge Bundy, also went on record stating that the decisions they made in regard to Black Studies would be open to discussion and possibly lead to turmoil. In his communication, he indicates that the grants will open the foundation to criticism and charges of social engineering. Additionally, Armsey stressed that "there are many theories of grant making, those that are at the moment causing them trouble is the dichotomy between whether the Ford Foundation should initiate or if they should respond."[11] In short, his concern was the conflict between those who advocated an integrationist perspective for Black Studies and those who supported the tenets of Black Power.

Armsey also said that "One school (the inside one usually) says initiate programs, design projects, set guidelines, do nothing that doesn't conform to predetermined criteria. The other (its principal spokesmen are often disappointed outsiders) says give the people what they want, respond but don't impose your own ideas on the clients."[12] He proceeds to suggest that whatever difficulty they are having making decisions regarding the grants reflects the same struggle playing itself out in the rest of the country vis à vis Black Power and racial reform. Armsey concludes that the Ford Foundation should not rely on one or the other position exclusively, but should "propose instead to be flexible, to recognize the fluidity of the problem and the volatility of the people and their wide divergence of views, to maneuver none of us into irreconcilable conflicts or inescapable positions."[13]

There was not total agreement within the Ford Foundation on the flexible strategy supported by Armsey. John Scanlon, in an interoffice memorandum entitled "Where the Rocks Are Likely to Come From" argued that the foundation, rather than exemplifying flexibility, was taking an approach that was likely to upset all involved parties. One the one hand, he suggested, their willingness to make grants to Black Studies programs signaled that "the Black experience is a worth-while subject for scholarly inquiry," a position that would run into opposition from conservative scholars and administrators who did not believe that a separate field of study organized around Black people deserved serious attention. On the other hand, he argued, the foundation would be criticized because the grants seemed to publicly reject the Black separatism called for by many Black students and community groups. Scanlon wrote that he believed "the angriest reaction will come from black militants seeking financial assistance for their own version of black studies programs. We have already said 'no' to a few of these that involved the creations of separate black colleges within predominantly white universities." Making clear his reasons for rejecting these requests, Scanlon added that, "In my judgment, requests of this kind that are based on the reparatist philosophy should be answered with a polite but firm 'no.'"[14]

Although Scanlon dismissed the ideological concerns of all

sides in the debate over the organizing principle of Black Studies as "ultimately trivial," he did not object to the idea that students be involved in program development, nor was he concerned about the possibility of the development of a full-fledged Black Studies major. He concluded that the Ford Foundation only needed to be concerned with the fact that "reputable scholars" would support their approach. He also made the point "that we are doing what we are doing not because we lack information, or conviction, or fortitude but because we believe prudence is the better part of valor." In order to ascertain that he was not misunderstood by Bundy, he concluded, "I agree wholeheartedly with Sir Arthur Lewis, Roy Wilkins, and other Negro leaders who maintain that separatism will simply not work in a pluralistic society."[15] If there was widespread support for diversifying curriculum, faculty, and student body, at the same time, the program officers were aware that their support of Black Studies, as a way to foster white racial sensitivity, was sure to cause some consternation.

While a good part of the debate over funding Black Studies was new and spoke to the particular political and cultural concerns of the parties involved, in fact, white philanthropic support of Black educational issues was longstanding.[16] Indeed, what the Ford Foundation did was reminiscent of a nineteenth-century educational endeavor underwritten by white philanthropic organizations. As in the 1960s, that effort would have long-term consequences and result in competing positions over the most beneficial way to prevent conflict by promoting long-term racial reconciliation. The issue of race and education in the United States was a well-discussed theme following the Civil War, and white philanthropic organizations stepped in to fund solutions. Indeed, in the wake of the war, the financially ruined South and white Southerners were forced to contemplate the most expedient way to rebuild their lives. At the same time, wealthy white Northerners were overwhelmingly interested in healing the rift between their Southern brethren and themselves.

One of the plans put forward by the United States government was the institutionalization of public education, whereby all school-aged children, Black and white, would be required to attend school. This plan, which was free of cost, immediately evinced a difference of opinion over the kind of education most befitting Black students. Backed by scientific racism and worried about national reconciliation, philanthropists and educators banded together to devise and finance a program for Black education that established a difference between what education could mean for Blacks and for whites. Black children were steered toward a system of industrial education or vocational training, and it was precisely for this type of education that philanthropists were able to raise and donate the largest amounts of money.

While in the late 1960s, the thinking and strategies linking the funding of Black education with white philanthropy were to take a different turn, using philanthropic funds to achieve social ends, in order to head off a racial crisis, was certainly not new. Within the context of public education, the education of former slaves came to dominate social discussion of the period, and white philanthropists offered financial help to implement various solutions. If by the 1960s, colleges and universities were interested in responding to the vast increase in African American students on their campuses, in the mid-nineteenth century, there was a concern about the masses of newly freed African Americans. A number of the leading ideologues proposed a solution to integrating newly freed Blacks into white culture, and American society responded to this crisis surrounding race in much the same way as McGeorge Bundy would do nearly a century later.

WHITE PHILANTHROPY AND BLACK EDUCATION: AN OVERVIEW

During the first few years following the end of the Civil War, white philanthropy responded to the post–Civil War hysteria over how to integrate Black people into the existing social order and maintain racial, economic, and political peace. Northerners rightfully saw their future bound up with the South, and Northern philanthropists and Southern thinkers formed an alliance in their position on Black education.[17] For some, the primary issue was the myth of lower Black intelligence. Others believed that the lack of economic opportunity for newly freed Blacks still living in the South should dictate the type of education they would be offered. In the eyes of many, both concerns could be addressed, if not solved, by implementing a vocational, or trade, curriculum. This idea caused Black intellectual W. E. B. Du Bois to sneer, in his highly influential work from 1903, *The Souls of Black Folks,* that such an education would relegate Blacks to be fit only as "hewers of wood and drawers of water," yet many, both Black and white, accepted this solution as the most politically, socially, and economically sound option for Black Southerners. Indeed it was a Black man—noted educator and political mover and shaker Booker T. Washington—who founded an occupational school, the Tuskegee Institute, dedicated to training newly freed African Americans to claim a relevant place in wartorn Southern society.

During the period following the war, varying individual philanthropists as well as philanthropic organizations consistently offered financial support for particular ideologies. This endeavor was not divorced from politics and the desire to both address racial tensions and come to a workable solution for avoiding a racial crisis. At the time, Southern whites feared that education for Blacks would provide African Americans with the means to eventually upset white supremacy. As a result, many whites in the South resisted Northern efforts at educational reform, even when couched in terms of industrial education, or educating Blacks to remain in their "place." In negotiating these racial tensions, Northern philanthropists often placated white Southerners by making sure that the educational reforms did not challenge white beliefs about race-based intelligence. However, philanthropists genuinely wanted to reform the South and believed this would lead to increased Black economic power and a lessening of the restrictive effects of Jim Crow. They kept their eyes on this particular prize, even if it was tied philosophically to industrial education for Black people.[18]

The vast majority of philanthropic support for Southern education in general and Black education in particular initially came from church groups in the North. Those efforts were overshadowed in 1902, however, when John D. Rockefeller established the General Education Board (GEB) and gave it $33 million to disburse between 1902 and 1912. Several other funds financed by philanthropic organizations with the same mission were established within the next fifteen years. Although there were certainly many who regarded these developments favorably, Methodist bishop Warren A. Candler sounded an alarm in a 1909 pamphlet entitled "Dangerous Donations and Degrading Doles." He warned that, "An educational trust [the GEB] has been formed, and is operating to control institutions of higher learning in the United States, and to dominate especially the colleges and universities in the South." He and others came to believe that there was a social agenda at work that endangered Southern autonomy and the social order, and that the Northern foundations sought to undermine the Southern system of race relations, "training negroes in the vain hope of social equality with whites."[19]

At the same time, although the response of white money to the racial tensions of the period is a study of the influence of the philanthropic foundations, it was also a period of time that revealed the limitations of their power. This resistance came from Black people who wanted more than a vocational education. In some ways, their desire to shape their educational experience was not that different from the demands and concerns of Black students in the 1960s. Indeed, at the beginning of the twentieth century, Black communities challenged the philanthropic foundations, expressing their own educational agendas in a variety of ways, including demands for Black teachers, resistance to any distinctive racial curricula, and, in some cases, support for independent Black schools. The millions of dollars contributed by African Americans also indicated their refusal to relinquish complete control of their schools to either the white South or distant philanthropists in the North. Nonetheless, it was the money available from and distributed by large white, Northern philanthropic concerns that came to shape future discussions about the direction and development of Black education. Foundations were able to institutionalize their perspectives on race and racial interaction and cooperation, through the schools, teachers, classes, and courses of study that they funded. As a result, Black education was affected by white philanthropy in ways both large and small, seen and unseen.[20]

However, as with the Ford Foundation's support of African American studies, while the supporters of industrial education had a particular vision of how white philanthropy should support the education of African Americans, their views and desires were not absolute. These ideologues wielded power and wealth that gave them a place at the table to decide the future of African Americans, but they were not the only players. Other whites, notably white missionary associations, supported a liberal arts education for African Americans and established schools for that purpose. African Americans also set up and funded schools with a liberal arts curriculum and more egalitarian notions of Black life in America. Further, some schools only pretended "to maintain an industrial education and hierarchical view of American racial relationships while relegating industrial arts to a corner of the curriculum. At universities like Fisk, students actually went on strike when the president attempted to alter the liberal arts focus of the curriculum in order to pander to white industrial interests."[21] However, to the extent that Northern philanthropists at the beginning of the twentieth century promoted a particular educational system based on race, they helped to perpetuate a racial gulf between whites and Blacks that continues to haunt present-day discussions of academic achievement in relation to race. It also permeates the field of Black studies. Within this historical context, the Ford Foundation at the end of the 1960s attempted to use philanthropic money to once again enter the debate over Black education, seeking to influence the future direction of racial relations.

THE FIRST ROUND OF GRANTS IN BLACK STUDIES

By the end of the 1960s, in an attempt to avoid supporting Black Studies programs based on an activist, separatist, or Black Nationalist viewpoint, Bundy—and by extension the Ford Foundation—firmly supported an organizational strategy of integration and curricular diversity for the new field. Their rationale was that Black Studies could help address Black social exclusion at the same time that the field educated whites about the literature, history, and culture of Black people. Their plan was designed to increase the acceptance of the subject's entrance into the academy, but not in a manner that would structurally strengthen and legitimize the actual programs and departments themselves. They certainly did not want Black Studies tied to efforts to promote Black Power. Indeed, while Bundy and the program officers were committed to legitimizing Black Studies, they primarily envisioned the new field as a tool that would lead to integrating the faculty and curriculum of traditional departments in higher education. As a result, instead of supporting a strategy that would lead to Black studies as an autonomous and permanent part of academe, the Foundation pursued a strategy that was most significantly concerned with gathering together and coordinating existing courses related to Black people.

Between 1969 and 1971, the Ford Foundation approved

over twenty Black Studies grants selected from more than one hundred applications. Twelve of the thirty-six applications from undergraduate programs were for funds to be used to restructure the present curriculum in order to include Black subjects. They were all fully funded. Two of the four grants for graduate programs likewise focused on overhauling and incorporating Black topics into existing graduate programs, and these were also funded. Four of the applications were from white research organizations such as the National Endowment for the Humanities, The American Education Institute, and the American Academy of Arts and Science. This last organization requested money to sponsor a conference on Black Studies specifically focused on the Black Diaspora. The conference proceedings were to be published in the association's magazine, *Daedalus*. They were all funded. Not one of the twelve applications from Black student groups, many asking for autonomous and separate colleges, departments, and programs of Black Studies, was awarded a grant.[22]

In 1969, five grants were awarded to Black colleges (Howard University, Lincoln University, Morgan State College, Jackson State College, Tuskegee University, and the Atlanta University Center). The same number were awarded to white colleges (Princeton, Yale, Rutgers, Vanderbilt, and Stanford). The historically Black Howard University asked for funding for a separate college of African American studies. Although that request was denied, they were granted money to coordinate the teaching of courses already offered at the institution, under the heading of Black Studies. The new department aimed to provide "a fundamental understanding of those economic, social, and political forces in the modern world which have shaped the contours of Negro experience." It also planned to "develop materials which supply an understanding of the cultural development of Negroes in a variety of historical and institutional settings in the New World." The historically Black Morgan State College asked for money and received a grant to compile and complete a syllabus project that would produce 13 one-semester collegiate syllabi in Black Studies that could be used as teaching materials for both their own classes and others'. In making a decision to fund that particular grant, foundation officers made a point of mentioning that "Morgan State does not offer a major in Afro-American studies, and does not intend to. Instead, it takes the view that the black experience should be infused into existing courses wherever it is appropriate to do so and that special courses dealing with the Negro and his contributions to American society should be offered only when there is a sufficient body of scholarly materials significant enough to warrant the creation of such courses."[23]

The grant to Morgan State totaled $150,000 over a two-year period, from 1969 to 1970, and was for the expressed purpose of completing a wide-ranging syllabus project on the topic of Black Studies in various disciplines, as a means of guiding the direction of many of the programs springing up around the country. Faculty and administrators who submitted the proposal believed that the project would help teachers and professors teach high-quality African American studies courses. The titles of the syllabi ran the gamut of disciplinary breadth: A Geography of the Negro in the City; The Ante-Bellum Protest Movement; Blacks in South, Central, and Caribbean America; The Negro in American Literature; The Negro and American Culture; The Negro in Art; The Negro in American History and Black Politics. It is particularly telling that the project took an additional year to be completed due to the "concerns of the Attorney General of Maryland that the contractual arrangements and agreements . . . not be in any way legally embarrassing to . . . the State."[24] In assessing whether the Ford Foundation should continue funding for the second year, the program officer in charge of that particular grant, John Scanlon, wrote that the president of the college "incidentally holds the same views as

Sir Arthur Lewis of Princeton about 'separatism' and 'black studies.' He said the separatist philosophy is black chauvinism and will lead to 'something worse than what we've been trying to get away from.' He also said that on many campuses Black students were 'being sold a bill of goods' by black militants who argue that nothing is relevant unless it is relevant to 'my blackness ...' "[25]

While the Ford Foundation may have been playing "catch up" to the aims and desires of white colleges and universities in regard to the implementation of Black Studies, it had a long history of supporting historically Black colleges and universities, and some of its officers wondered if they should confine their efforts to supporting these institutions. At least one program officer wondered why, if the intent of the foundation was to provide support for Black education, they couldn't simply proceed as planned. Indeed, John Scanlon strongly believed that the most effective way to further the cause of racial justice in higher education was to continue to primarily support historically Black colleges and universities. In his report to the Ford Foundation on educational initiatives for minorities, Scanlon argued that "Although the Supreme Court decision of 1954 outlawed segregation in higher education as well as in public schools, most colleges and universities throughout the country dragged their feet throughout the Fifties and early Sixties in admitting black students." Given this reality, Scanlon asserted that, although the numbers of Black students on white college campuses continued to rise, it was important for the Ford Foundation to remember that a majority of Black students still attended Black colleges. He then urged the foundation to vigorously support "the eighty-six degree granting colleges and universities that had been established to serve Black Americans," as they were the best avenue into higher education for thousands of Black students in the South, as well as for many in other regions of the country. The Ford Foundation's support for "Black students attending Black colleges was significant between the early 1950s through the mid 1970s. During that period, they awarded more than $250 million to both Black colleges and to organizations dedicated to advancing opportunities for African Americans in higher education. The United Negro College Fund received $1 million dollars in 1953 alone."[26] Although they continued to vigorously support Black studies at Black colleges, this support did not stop their new plan of funding Black Studies on white college campuses. Sometimes Ford was able to provide support for both at the same time.

Indeed, in one of the grants, the funds were to be shared among Rutgers University, Princeton University, and the historically Black Lincoln University. All three schools were planning to start Black Studies programs in the fall of 1969 but found that there were not enough faculty members available for all of them. The grant was awarded so that the "three institutions, which are only about one hundred miles apart, will establish procedures which will allow a faculty member of one institution to teach one or more courses or seminars at one of the others." While Lincoln was much smaller and less well known than either Rutgers or Princeton, the foundation officers informed Bundy that it should be funded if at all possible because "since its founding in 1854 it has had close ties with Africa...over the years since then hundreds of African students have graduated from Lincoln. Two of them later became presidents of African nations (Kwame Nkrumah of Ghana and Nnamdi Azikiwe of Nigeria)...."[27] Finally, in addition to Lincoln's illustrious history, the Ford Foundation was particularly interested in including the university because it planned on beginning an institute that would coordinate existing courses and develop new ones that might serve as a model for Rutgers, Princeton, and other institutions.

Despite widespread support for the idea of Black Studies, some in the Ford Foundation viewed the foundation's support as only necessary for the short term. In 1972, after the first round of grants had been approved and were then up for review, one of the Ford Foundation's vice presidents, Harold Howe II, a former United States commissioner of education in the Johnson Administration, circulated a memo suggesting that the sum total of the organization's support should be limited to the thirty or so grants awarded between 1969 and 1970. Indeed, Howe would say that he was satisfied with the progress they had made in regard to Black Studies and suggest that they "call it a day" as far as their involvement with the new field was concerned.[28] Although they clearly chose not to heed that advice, they did continue to separate themselves from any hint of militancy. This practice was abundantly evident in the funding of one particular grant awarded among that first group. It was given to Vanderbilt University and, although it initially fit firmly within the foundation's goals for a depoliticized as well as interdisciplinary organizational model for Black Studies, it looked to administrators as if it was veering off in another direction.

In many ways, the history of Vanderbilt's Afro-American Studies department is similar to that of many other schools that started programs without significant student or community unrest. Although there was no ugly student strike, an interracial committee of faculty members on the campus organized themselves into the Race Relations Committee, and a group of students named the Afro-American Association submitted a proposal for an Afro-American Studies program. The program was suitably interdisciplinary in scope, organized so that students would major in any one of five disciplines while taking enough courses in the program to receive a certificate, or minor, in Black Studies when they graduated. The courses were, for the most part, already offered at Vanderbilt, and the only new offerings that the program needed funding for were a course on the government's policy toward racial minorities and another on Black theater. The chair of the faculty Race Relations Committee, Charles Izzard, wrote to the Ford Foundation to request $47,000 in funding for start-up costs and to fund a series of seminars that they hoped would lead to an "interuniversity consortium" on race.[29]

Upon receiving funding from Ford and beginning a program of Afro-American Studies, the university hired Akbar Muhammad, a graduate student in history, to chair it. Having already published in a number of history journals and completed a graduate degree at the University of Edinburgh in Scotland, Muhammad was working on his doctorate, with a focus on Islamic history. He was also the son of Elijah Muhammad, the leader of the Black nationalist religious group the Nation of Islam; however, he had already separated himself from both his father and the Nation of Islam at the point and which he accepted the position. The first year he was director of the program, instead of offering the members of the multiracial Race Relations Committee the opportunity to teach the general social science courses they had proposed, with titles such as "Philosophy of the Social World," "Human Evolution and Human Race," and "The Sociology of Poverty," he organized and taught his own courses. There was a decidedly different slant to them, what with titles like "Introduction to the Black Experience & Black Protest," "The African Origins of Black Americans and the Slave Trade," and "Black Historians and Black History." Vanderbilt's assistant dean, Elton Hinshaw, complained to Ford, "Since my last report in February, Mr. Akbar Muhammad has taken control of the Afro-American Studies program. He is 'blackwashing' some of the courses and restructuring the curriculum."[30]

Muhammad was perhaps unaware that anyone in the administration had characterized his leadership of the program in a negative light, when, in March of 1971, he wrote to the dean of the college to request that he intervene with Ford to allow a portion of the grant money Vanderbilt had received to be used to fund a study of Afro-American Studies Programs proposed by a

Black senior in the sociology department. He noted that "very little academic research has been carried out with a view to determining the pros and cons of Black Studies, its structure and content." The one study that he mentioned had taken place in 1970 and had not been published. In any case, he noted, "in view of recent changes in programs at various colleges and universities," the findings in that previously conducted survey were "fast becoming outdated."[31]

Muhammad suggested that the university should support his request in part because it would put Vanderbilt in a good light, but also because "There is a desire on the part of Black Studies directors and chairmen for a detailed analysis of these programs throughout the United States." He noted that other directors had approached him asking about the organizational details of his program and that he had approached others asking about how they had structured their programs. He went on to add that the survey for which he was attempting to secure funding would "through comparison, serve as a basis for improving programs" around the country.[32]

Despite the fact that Ford generally looked quite favorably on proposals that aimed to gather and disseminate information between groups of academics in the academy, in this instance, the organization denied the request and declined to support the project. The reason they gave was that they could not approve funding for projects not originally included in the original application. One wonders if they saw a difference between gathering and disseminating information in general and doing so when the result would possibly have led to clearer communication, planning, and organizing on the part of Black Studies directors for the purpose of moving the field more fully toward autonomy and academic legitimacy. Whatever their reasoning, when he heard of their decision, Mr. Muhammad thanked the foundation for the financial assistance they had been willing to give and pointed to what the foundation money had helped accomplish.

He concluded by noting that "despite all the progress, the program still had problems being accepted at Vanderbilt."[33] This was the case for a majority of Black Studies programs and departments around the country.

LOOKING BACK AND WONDERING: SURVEYING THE FIELD FIVE YEARS LATER

In 1974, almost exactly five years after the first programs were created, the U.S. Department of Health, Education, and Welfare commissioned the Institute for Services to Education to do a study on Black Studies and the issues that seemed to affect the institutional survival of the new field. This is one of the few published reports on the state of Black Studies not funded by the Ford Foundation. It sounded a warning.

The commission validated many of the assertions of Bundy and Ford program officers and made clear that autonomy versus separatism was, years after the first programs were founded, still a troubling concern for many professors in Black Studies programs. Although initiated as academic innovations on many campuses and hailed as the first step in a coming revolution by students on still other campuses, "Inherent in the survival of Black Studies programs is an apparent contradiction. Black Studies programs during this time in large measure grew out of Black student demands for a different kind of option in their educational development. As the programs emerged, however, it became obvious that their acceptance as respectable academic additions would depend on the extent to which their structures, purposes and course offerings approximated traditional programs." Although described as innovative, most were dependent on traditional departments for support, funding, and legitimacy, and that reality, while fully supported by Ford, was having a destabilizing impact on the field as a whole. The report was prompted by "the need to provide critical information about the development and implementation of a variety of somewhat new programs which addressed vital social, cross cultural and historical issues and problems in American education."[34] By acknowledging that the field of Black Studies was relevant to education in America and that the programs served a number of needs that interested the Department of Education, the report provides a critical indication of how and why the struggles and debates in African American Studies mattered to colleges at large.

Beginning in 1972, almost four years after the first programs began, the main tasks of the study were to formulate a general working definition of Black Studies, ascertain the purpose, nature, and function of the twenty-nine representative programs, and identify the major issues associated with the development and implementation of Black Studies programs in the academy. Interestingly, as this was one of the earliest and most complete studies to offer an overview of Black Studies, it is crucial to note that one of the first questions the committee took up was the relation of violence to the reasons the schools started their programs. Over half of the thirty department and program chairs surveyed said that there were reasons other than violence at the center of the choice to begin a Black Studies program, and a majority of them had a fairly traditional view of the role of the field in relation to Black communities.[35] Many of the questions addressed the issue of ownership of the new field, and issues of politics, legitimacy, and intellectual viability loomed large.

One of the first things that the commission writers discovered was that their discussion soon evolved into what they described as an "intellectual free-for-all." In addition to probing into the nature of the new field, they inquired about the relationship between Black Studies and traditional fields, and wondered if an absence of a defined methodology meant that Black Studies should be centered in a traditional discipline where an established "proof system" already existed. They also asked if Black Studies should be regarded as an agent of "critical reform"—that is, if there was a special epistemological frame that should define Black Studies, and if the field would add to, or otherwise impact, critical inquiry. They also wondered if Black Studies should be its own major, and if so, whether it should be utilitarian or intellectual in nature. In short, the commission asked the hard questions that went to the heart of what the field could offer and might become. They did, however, all agree that the one question they need not ask was if Black Studies could be a field, if it had enough of a history and bibliography to sustain the intellectual endeavor that a new field of study requires.

The commission found that the first and foremost goal of the programs was to provide an understanding of the life, history, and culture of African Americans, with the hope of providing proof of the contributions, and therefore worth, of Black people to civilization. The second goal was to include the development of the "tools of inquiry," and research about the "Black experience was, within this context seen as the goal of Black Studies." The third most common justification for the program was for the purpose of social change, in that the programs sought to provide the tools and knowledge that would allow students to "compete favorably in the greater American and International society." The fourth common objective was to promote a Pan-African focus among people of "African heritage wherever they are found," and the fifth most cited reason for having Black Studies was to deal with the pervasive nature of racism in American society.

It is particularly interesting to note that the government report stated that those in the field were beginning to question the role of white philanthropic organizations:

By selecting certain programs for funding while denying support to others, government agencies and foundations could manipulate the political orientation of these programs and the direction of academic research. With hun-

dreds of such programs competing for limited funds, effective control of the future of Black Studies was thereby
shifted away from Black scholars and students, and instead...to the funding agencies—college administrations, government and foundations. Departments that
were thought by the establishment to be dangerously independent or radical could thus be crippled or destroyed
without the necessity of resorting to violent repression.[36]

This was certainly a very real, though unintended, consequence of the strategy pioneered by Bundy and the Ford Foundation. Although clearly committed to a particular rationale for
the new field, internally the Ford Foundation discussed the field
of Black Studies as constituting a step in a larger plan to address
America's "Negro Problem." However, if, in the past, the foundation had funded groups and organizations whose leaders, in
an effort to right racial wrongs, spoke what McGeorge Bundy
termed in the *Ford Foundation Annual Report* for 1968 "justifi-
ably angry words," one year later, anger, militancy, and power
were no longer tenable in relation to Black Studies, at least as far
as the Ford Foundation was concerned. As a result, as opposed
to funding the field in a manner that could lead to the accusation
of promoting political insurgency and racial unrest, they proposed funding Black Studies solely as a means to desegregate
higher education. Black Studies, as one researcher indicated,
"could be a tool for racial equality as long as it was conceptual-
ized as an extension or reform of American academia." This was
a significant shift from the position Ford had taken just months
before.[37] However, given Bundy's practice of declaring, when
questioned about difficult positions, "Look, I'm settled about
this. Let's not talk about it any more. I may be wrong but I'm
not in doubt," it was surely a shift that he intended to make and
believed was the right thing to do.[38]

MAYBE WRONG, BUT NEVER IN DOUBT

In many ways, McGeorge Bundy was both a man of his time and a man ahead of his time. When he assumed the presidency of Ford in 1966, he fully believed that, if not addressed, racial conflict was sure to tear America apart. Two societies, one white and the other Black, had developed and were clearly separate and undeniably unequal. As a man of his time, he could not have helped but know that race was an issue in need of sustained attention, and given his history with higher education, it was only logical that he would seek to address the issue within the confines of academia. As a man ahead of his time, he was able to offer a complex analysis of race in America by relying on the work of Black scholars, intellectuals, and academics in order to deepen his understanding of America as a whole. Indeed, it was his readings of and conversations with such men as W. E. B. Du Bois, Roy Wilkins, Ralph Bunch, Bayard Rustin, and Martin Luther King Jr. that enabled him to write "the destiny of the Negro in America is to be both Negro and American." With Du Bois's formulation of duality firmly in mind, Bundy went on to suggest, "I think we make a mistake when we attempt to compare the white/black relation with those between the Yankees and the Irish, or the Wasps and the Jews, or any other of the dozens of conflict-laden relations that have marked our social history." He concluded that those comparisons would not work because the racial conflict in America between Blacks and whites is "so much deeper and bigger that it has a different order of meaning."[39]

While the field of Black Studies came to be implemented in a manner that openly acknowledged fissures in the histories, present circumstances, and curricula of universities and colleges, what it would mean to Black students, white university officials and administrators, and Black teachers and community members was not always apparent. There were fundamental differences in what many thought the field was capable of doing, and even disagreement over whether it needed to exist at all. In ways that could be considered both positive and negative, the "Black Studies Movement" forced colleges and universities to rethink "who they admitted as students and by what standards they made their admission decisions." Stephen Alan Jones, a scholar who has written on the legacy of Black Studies, points out that in many ways, the legacy of Black Studies is that it challenged the very foundations of university process by "questioning the entire structure of scholarly endeavor, what is researched, what is taught, and how the whole intellectual undertaking is organized."[40] If this is true, we cannot know how much more successful Black Studies might have been in its transformational impulses if allowed the funding and given the encouragement to go even further.

While it is not evident how well acknowledged the legacy of Black Studies is within academia, it is undeniably true that the field had an impact on universities from the moment it was first instituted. As Jones has argued, "first and foremost, Black Studies challenged American higher education to open itself to real—not merely token—participation by African Americans." Given the fact that Black enrollment on white campuses had begun to grow after 1960, but that the growth was what Jones terms "painfully slow," Black Studies provided a focal point for Black activists' demands that white campuses recruit and retain increased numbers of African American students and faculty. Jones proceeds to observe that in this particular regard, Black Studies was an extension of the civil rights movement, pressing colleges and universities to assume the democratic ideals at the very heart of America.[41] It is also the case that the Ford Foundation intervened in a particular manner so as to ensure that it would not be easy for Black Studies as a field to evolve beyond its utilitarian function on many college campuses and begin to analyze the complicated nature of race in America's past, present, and future. However, even despite the lack of support, that is precisely what Black Studies was capable of offering then, and that type of analysis is what the field offers America today.

The challenge presented to colleges and universities by Black Studies was substantive. While in the period before the 1960s, the university saw its role as passing on knowledge that was agreed to be significant, most institutions did not believe that they were responsible for fostering racial harmony through the enactment of Black Studies programs. That changed by the middle of the twentieth century, and college administrators came to view racial integration as their responsibility. The specifics of what it meant to integrate, the terms by which it should occur, and the timing for when it should happen were topics needing addressing in the late 1960s, especially within the university context. If universities had once been elite bastions where knowledge was produced and shared in isolationist splendor, by the late 1960s, it was obvious that the tower's foundations, ivory and all, had been questioned, found wanting, and shaken to their core.

The demands placed on universities to become more responsive and "relevant" to their students were widespread, and in no way confined to the area of race. Given the cultural context of the time, which included generational tensions, opposition to the Vietnam War, the struggle for Black rights, and increasingly vocal and strident calls for women's rights as well, university administrators found themselves at the center of these cultural and social issues, and they were struggling to hold on to their traditional roles. At the same time, they wanted to respond to the shifts taking place in American culture. For many located within academia, as well as outside of it, Black Studies was a means to a greater end. This was especially true for the Ford Foundation, and they understood that "Whatever we set as our targets, we cannot hit them without the help of universities."[42] It is then no wonder that cracks and fissures developed as the field struggled to bear the weight of so many deeply significant expectations.

The lessons Ford learned from their willingness to finance Black Power proponents in the Stokes election and during the Ocean-Hill Brownsville strike, coupled with the sting of the resulting backlash, shaped how Ford approached funding for "the Negro Problem" from that point onward. Black Studies was to be a clearinghouse through which Black faculty, Black texts, and Black students could be funneled to traditionally white disciplines such as history, English, and sociology. As a result, at the same time that Black Studies was institutionalized at the college level, a particular political perspective was also established that would later undermine the discipline's stability and coherent development. In an article ruminating abut the overall relationship of philanthropic organizations to race, Alice O'Connor, one of the Ford Foundation's former program officers, argued that "liberal philanthropy has most effectively used detached, 'scientific' research to pursue an ideological agenda that has had profound political consequences. The overall thrust of that philanthropic agenda has been to neutralize race as a political and economic as well as a social and cultural issue."[43]

In regard to the relationship between the early institutionalization of Black Studies and the meaning of such programs to Black communities, according to English professor and cultural critic Gerald Early, "The foundation for black studies was highly problematic." Indeed, he adds, "Black Studies at the white university was a bourgeois act of integration, further alienating black professors and black communities that could not support them."[44] If so, we are left to wonder about the significance, meaning, and function of Black Studies within higher education today. That topic is the theme of the next chapter.

5

THE LEGACY IN THE PRESENT

> Perhaps Black Studies at the white university will eventu-
> ally force everyone—Black and white—to look at what
> Black institutions are, how they are meant to function,
> and the difficulty of maintaining them. And perhaps
> white institutions will learn to work in the best interests
> of Blacks as well.[1]

While Black Studies was initially discussed by those both within
and outside of the academy as primarily having institutional, as
opposed to intellectual, significance, the cover of the *Atlantic
Monthly* magazine's April 1995 issue made a very different
claim. The publication announced that America's "New Intellectuals," despite having been pronounced dead by the press and
various other cultural commentators, were in fact back on the
scene. Readers looking at the cover were both shown and told
that not only were they back, but that now "they're black."[2]
The article's cover pictured an unmistakably Black fist raised in
a Black Power–era salute, a symbol of the field's historical origins. The fist clutched a fountain pen, a symbol for intellectual
pursuits, indicating the change that had taken place in the past
twenty years. The article described a "new" breed of African
American intellectual and a "new" mode of racial thinking that
had produced a "new" focus for the field of African American
Studies. Those heralded in the article were so described because
they "thought less exclusively about the meaning of 'blackness'
and more inclusively about what it means to be an African

American—taking pains to scrutinize both sides of the hyphen."[3] Despite the explicit attempts to remake its symbolism, the image on the cover of the magazine represents Black Power and is drawn from a period when Blackness as a revolutionary, corrective, or disruptive enterprise defined the field of Black Studies in many minds.

What is interesting about this article is its assertion that there is something particularly new about African American intellectuals thinking and writing deeply about race and its complex relationship to American culture. W. E. B. Du Bois wrote eloquently on the topic from the turn of the last century until his death in August of 1963. James Baldwin's analysis of the relationships between love, anger, race, and America's core organizational structures established him as an intellectual giant and skilled wordsmith with few equals, white or Black. Toni Morrison's intellectual contributions to American letters have been honored with both a Pulitzer Prize and the Nobel Prize for Literature; in both her essays and fiction, she has explored relationships between social power and race, both historically and in America's present. None wrote exclusively about what it meant to Black, but rather about how race was a central feature of American identity for whites and Blacks, indeed for our country as a whole. Those are just three examples, all very well known. There are numerous other African American intellectuals and academics whose work over the centuries has taken as its subject just the type of topic that the magazine article describes as "new."

How then to explain the article's assertion that it was not until 1995 that the field matured to the point where those within it no longer "thought exclusively" about Blackness, and instead thought more expansively about what it means to be American within the context of racial identity? Perhaps that perception is best explained by a lack of knowledge about the scholarship in the field, and the overwhelming association between African

American Studies and Black protest, dating from its formative years. That history has served to obscure the *intellectual* utility of African American Studies in favor of a narrative that emphasizes its use as a tool to recruit a diverse faculty and student body to predominantly white institutions. The problem, as historian Nell Irvin Painter has written, is that "the silent, even unconscious assumption still prevails that black studies and black faculty members suit each other perfectly, because the field is simple and the people are not so smart." She adds, "The reluctance to accept that blackness and intelligence are not mutually exclusive affects black faculty members, whatever their field, and it affects faculty members in black studies, whatever their personal racial identity."[4]

In short, the success of the Ford Foundation's strategy of funding Black Studies programs has created a complex situation wherein institutions continue to use the field in order to diversify their institutions, but very often, the preponderance of Black people in and around African American Studies programs, and their absence in other departments in those institutions, unfairly mark the field as an affirmative action program. While individual faculty members within African American Studies may be viewed as intelligent, the field—usually structured as an interdisciplinary entity where faculty hold appointments in both traditional departments and within African American Studies—is rarely viewed as the vibrant site of intellectual activity that it is. This is part of the legacy of its past that will have an impact on the future of African American Studies within higher education.

Moreover, by the 1990s, there were at least two noteworthy developments in African American Studies. Black Studies became something now known as African American Studies, and affirmative action policies made African American faculty far more central to this new field than the "rowdy" Black students who had come to define its earlier manifestation. If racial integration was at the heart of efforts to institutionalize Black Studies in the 1970s, and separatism the accusation hurled at those who argued for its independence, by the 1990s, popular views of the field were defined by assimilation and the charge was that of an unfair racial advantage due to the relationship between affirmative action and Black Studies. Further, in the early 1970s, as Nell Irvin Painter recalls of Black Studies, "Many black academics entered our profession with an intellectual mission: to correct erroneous and pernicious notions about African-Americans. Our scholarship is often a scholarship of struggle, concentrating on our own, stigmatized group," but by the 1990s, according to Gerald Early, Black faculty associated with the field—by then called African American Studies—no longer desired "outsider" status. He believes African American Studies had become "obsessed with wanting intellectual respectability, with being taken seriously by whites as a scholarly enterprise that produces genuine, peer-reviewed, rigorously researched work. It wants, above all else, to have honor, an important need for members of oppressed minorities."[5] Although a desire for "honor" and the ability to do "rigorously researched work" do not preclude the intellectual mission Painter describes, the two are clearly describing different perspectives on what African American Studies has to offer the academy. At times, those perspectives are at odds with each other.

Because of the success of the Ford Foundation's conception of Black Studies as a means of diversification, most of the departments and programs that were established came to mirror Ford's suggested strategies for dealing with the problem of racial crisis in higher education. However, those organizational strategies would become as much a cause of concern and contention as the legacy of the association between Black Power and Black studies.

TRAVELS IN TIME: BLACK STUDIES, AFRICAN AMERICANS, AND AFFIRMATIVE ACTION

Clearly, African American Studies has had great success as a field and is acknowledged as important. As the *Atlantic Monthly* article also made clear, intellectual production in 1995 was spearheaded by African Americans in African American Studies departments on elite college campuses. These developments were surely a validation of the strategy McGeorge Bundy and the Ford Foundation had crafted twenty years earlier to address the Black presence within higher education. At the same time, the shift in nomenclature and the focus on faculty, as opposed to students, indicate a racial concern on college campuses that is markedly different from the one the field was first institutionalized to address. Indeed, in addressing race-based programs designed to increase the presence of racial minorities on college campuses, conservative African American commentator Thomas Sowell has written, "While integration was the goal, affirmative action has tended to re-segregate. Even academically strong black students get tarred with the brush of being 'quota' students while having weaker students in elite schools has led to the development of black studies programs."[6] The abrupt association he makes between weak African American students and the development of Black Studies programs may be questionable, but this perception has continued to gain traction among self-described Black conservatives. As Supreme Court justice Clarence Thomas has declared, "universities...talk the talk of multiculturalism and racial diversity in the courts but walk the walk of tribalism and racial segregation on their campuses— through minority-only student organizations, separate minority housing opportunities, separate minority student centers, even separate minority-only graduation ceremonies."[7] The relationship between affirmative action and Black Studies, while initially embraced and actively struggled for, has, twenty years later, become a source of contention, if not outright frustration for some African Americans in those institutions.

The news, however, is not all troubling. At colleges and universities around the country, the existence of African American Studies as a discipline is accepted and viewed as a useful tool by white administrators. Gone is the hesitancy, soul searching, and white guilt so much a part of the early history of Black Studies' institutionalization. At the same time, gone too is the student demand and the sense of expectancy on the part of interested African American community members and groups. Indeed, Black people, conservative and otherwise, were, by the 1990s, as apt to question the usefulness and racial rationale for ghettoizing the study of people of African descent, as they were to hail the founding of a program as a positive development, and few in Black communities watch with bated breath as announcements are made about hiring decisions in Black Studies programs. However, even without the benefit of community racial pressure, by 1987, a Ford study on the state of African American Studies found that a majority of white administrators enthusiastically supported the field. The report points out that for such administrators, the purpose of African American Studies involved what they termed "institutional expediency." The nature of that expediency had changed in the twenty-year period since the founding of the field, however.[8]

While in the 1970s, the push for Black Studies was tied to an influx of Black students and a desire to respond to the calls for "relevant" classes and educational experiences for them, by the 1990s, African American Studies was described by the administrators interviewed as useful in an effort to address a shrinking African American student body. Indeed, many universities were by the late 1980s enrolling noticeably fewer African American students in their institutions, and the report found that university administrators were "increasingly using strong black studies departments, programs, centers and institutes as recruitment devices."[9] While perhaps first noticed in the late 1980s, this was a trend that had been evolving since 1977 and involved the cuts in federal aid during and since Ronald Reagan's presidency. In the thirty-plus years since the founding of the first African American Studies programs, federal grants and scholarships have decreased over 65 percent, with more cuts on the horizon.[10]

This circumstance has disproportionately affected African American students, and as a result of their falling numbers in higher education, college administrators renewed their efforts to establish African American Studies programs as a means to stem the slide, according to the Ford report. What the report fails to mention is the fact that, even when they are present on campuses and have the opportunity, fewer Black students are actually taking courses in African American Studies. This is a trend that has been occurring for some time and that speaks to an unexamined change in the role of African American Studies on college campuses around the country.

One of the few studies to track Black enrollment in Black or African American Studies courses found that at a handful of institutions such as Duke, Brown, and Dartmouth, between 40 and 60 percent of all Black students took at least one course in the field, but at other institutions such as Cornell, Emory, and the University of Virginia, the figure dropped to between 14 and 20 percent. Further, according to a survey conducted by the *Journal of Blacks in Higher Education,* at least among Black students, "Black Studies is an unpopular major." The article notes that less than 1 percent of African American college students nationwide major in the field, and in 2000, more Black students took classes and earned degrees in mathematics, physics, engineering, biology, psychology, computer science, English, and home economics. All are fields where Black people are still described as underrepresented. On some campuses, more white students took African American Studies courses than did Black students.[11]

What to make of the fact that most Black students do not take a majority of classes in African American Studies? How could a field with such limited ability to attract Black students be so consistently viewed as a primary means of attracting such students? Why is the association between attracting Black students and an African American Studies program still so strong, despite all the evidence to the contrary? When will African American Studies be valued more for its intellectual output than its ability to recruit Black students? These are but a few of the questions that come to mind when thinking about the contemporary meaning of African American Studies programs in higher education, and the answers to them point to shifting racial politics today.

An underexplored drop in the numbers of Black students on white college campuses, a growing dependence on an ill-advised strategy by administrators to support African American Studies primarily as a means of attracting Black students, an inability to account for the increasing presence of white students in Black Studies courses, and the added pressures of funding, intellectual relevance, and connections with African American people and communities outside of academia have all placed added pressures on the field. Indeed, many have wondered if it would fold under the weight of so many different types of expectations. Within that context, knowing when, how, and why African American Studies came to be is an important step toward understanding the present and future of such programs, as well as the nature of racial interactions and understandings on contemporary college campuses.

Given that by the 1990s the field was struggling to attract Black students, we can conclude that "utility" might have functioned in similar ways during the two periods, but that the results clearly differed to a great extent. There is clearly a connection between utilizing a field of study to address a particular racial group on college campuses and utilizing it to address those whom administrators are attempting to attract. In both instances, the study of people of African descent is organized so as to attract, be attractive to, and to primarily teach Black students. What is clearly missing is an acknowledgment of the significance of the intellectual work that takes place within African American Studies.

The tale Black Studies programs' historical presence told in the 1970s about access to higher education for African Americans has been replaced in our contemporary period with a more complex and constantly shifting understanding about race and racial integration. It also tells us something about the result of the high-stakes battle to achieve racial balance on college campuses in our post–civil rights era. Indeed, there is a "now widely held view that any race-based amelioration constitutes a form of reverse discrimination" and "indicates that the public effort to secure social, civil, and political redress for racially aggrieved communities has reached an historic impasse, if not end."[12] In short, the history of the Ford Foundation's involvement in and funding for Black Studies still has significant ramifications for our experience of and discussions about race, integration, and affirmative action policies in higher education as we begin a new millennium.

FORD, BLACK STUDENTS, AND THE POST–CIVIL RIGHTS ERA

Between 1969, when the first round of grants were made to fund African American Studies programs, and the late 1990s, the Ford Foundation donated over twenty million dollars to both graduate and undergraduate programs and to departments of African American studies. Over one million additional dollars was granted by the foundation to support the editing, archiving, and collection of oral history information concerning Black or African American Studies.[13] Although Ford had made an initial commitment to over one dozen programs, they believed that the money was merely for start-up and that colleges and universities would assume the responsibility for funding Black Studies on their campuses once the initial three-year grant had expired. This was clearly Ford's thinking, but on at least one occasion, one of their program officers reported widespread dismay on the part of Black Studies directors and college administrators that this was the case. None seemed aware that Ford was not planning to fund Black Studies indefinitely.[14] For those programs not funded by Ford in either the short or the long term, issues of student interest and enrollment numbers were of primary significance. Unfortunately, after the initial demand and overwhelming interest and implementation of Black Studies between 1969 and 1971, there was a rather sharp decline in interest on the part of Black students, and program creation also declined.

Indeed, by 1974, in addition to the problems with curriculum, qualified faculty, and relationships with traditional departments, there was a more general concern that these programs would become extinct for lack of enrollment. Further, it was evident to both faculty and administrators that there was a pressing need for money to sustain the new field, and without additional income sources or sustained interest and enrollment by Black students, the prospect of Black Studies was bleak. According to a report authored by Nathan Huggins for the Ford Foundation, summarizing the reasons why enrollment across the country dropped so noticeably by 1974, "Born, as these programs were, out of campus crises, in an era of highly charged rhetoric, unconditional demands, and cries for revolution, it was difficult for them to shake that style and reputation."[15]

The reasons for the decline in student interest were many, he claimed, but the most pressing were: "(1) students, both black and white, increasingly turned from political to career concerns; (2) the atmosphere in many courses was hostile and antagonistic to white students; (3) many of the courses lacked substance and academic rigor; and (4) campus communities had been exhausted by the rhetoric, bombast, and revolutionary ideology that still permeated many of these courses and programs."[16] At the same time, one report on enrollment in Black Studies courses found that, in addition to issues with the organization of particular programs, the fact that the Black middle class expanded exponentially in the 1970s produced a generation of Black students on predominantly white campuses who, by the 1990s, were "highly focused on courses" that would "lead to better incomes. And huge numbers of black college students enroll in college to train for a career in the business world. For a very large number of African American college students, a degree in black studies is seen as a dead-end street, unless of course one has an ambition to teach in the field."[17] One wonders why the same concern does not prevent more students from majoring in English, religion, or history.

It is understandable that the interests of Black students might shift in a twenty-year period, and the seeming relationship between economic prosperity and the decline in enrollment surely suggests that American culture had lifted some of the earlier barriers to African American advancement in some areas. Still, what is interesting about that shift in perspective and interest by Black students is the fact that it did not influence the thinking of college administrators, who continued to view Black Studies as a recruiting tool for Black students. Indeed, it would appear that they hardly noticed that the real result of their efforts was an increase in the numbers of Black faculty, who were often the only Black faculty with whom white students might come into contact. Tellingly, and perhaps alarmingly, according to the survey of Black Studies programs and departments around the country conducted by Ford, at a majority of the institutions the interviewers visited in the late 1980s, the "only critical mass of black faculty working at many of these institutions" was associated with Black Studies. These findings are confirmed by historian Nell Irvin Painter, who has noted that, "In predominantly white institutions, students and administrators—of all backgrounds—commonly equate black faculty members and black studies."[18]

It would seem then that Black Studies has become a means of ensuring that Black faculty are hired, not a means to provide relevant and much needed insight and intellectual contribution and critique. While perhaps a small and seemingly unimportant matter, this shift in perspective is both significant and instructive regarding our post–civil rights era. Indeed, as Nikhil Singh has written:

> The unraveling of the social and political consensus that enabled the limited reforms of the earlier period has exposed the shaky political, institutional, and ideological foundations on which much racial progress has been built. . . . For a brief period, the demands and critiques of black intellectuals, activists, and masses of black people who took to the streets could not be ignored. . . . Yet in the crucible fired by the clash of black protest and white supremacy, . . . national integration, let alone racial justice and equality, has been the exception more often than the rule.[19]

The fact that, by 1987, in the minds of white administrators, African American studies was a means to attract Black students—despite evidence to the contrary—is clearly a legacy from the earlier period of McGeorge Bundy and the Ford Foundation. The zeal with which African American Studies was embraced had seemingly run its course by the mid-1970s. However, as Black Studies became African American Studies, a new meaning came to the fore that was as revealing about its historical significance as what had occurred previously. Indeed, as Black Studies became African American Studies, race, intellectual production, and integration in higher education would take a different slant entirely.

STORIES FROM THE FRONT LINES: AFRICAN AMERICAN
STUDIES IN CONTEMPORARY AMERICA

In 1995, fresh out of graduate school, I began my first academic job as an assistant professor of English and director of African American Studies at the University of Missouri-Kansas City (UMKC). Not only was I offered the position of director of African American Studies, but, given the fact that there was no such program in existence when I was hired, I was also charged with creating a program of study leading to a certificate, or minor, at the school. There was no budget or staff set aside for this endeavor. There were, however, repeated assurances about unlimited financial support from the school's administration. I was able to overlook the lack of a definite budget because there appeared to be substantial enthusiasm for beginning an organized program in Black Studies. It was high time, those who interviewed me kept repeating, that the school do something about its lack of diversity and its rocky relationships with "the Black Community" in Kansas City. Besides, I heard from faculty and administrators alike, attracting students interested in African American Studies should be relatively easy, because the public school system was over 80 percent African American. Most importantly, my soon to be new colleagues smilingly told me, I was going to be hired with two other Black faculty people, so I wouldn't be lonely and would have ready-made faculty people to participate in what was sure to be a successful experiment.

I now know that the job owed a debt to the history and legacy of Black Studies as a primary tool to achieve racial integration in institutions of higher education. I also now realize that Black Studies is often looked at by administrators as a way to address racial crisis. In my case, unbeknownst to me, there was the threat of a lawsuit charging racial discrimination at the institution. Once news of the newly instituted African American Studies program was made public, along with the fact of the hiring of three Black faculty people, the suit was dropped. Overall,

the advent of African American Studies at UMKC and the fact
that I was hired to direct it are, in a variety of ways, testament
to the efficacy of Ford's strategies to foster racial inclusion in
higher education. I know this now, but I was not aware of it
then.

At the time, the title of director of anything rang with ego-
stroking import in my newly minted PhD ears, and I did not initially question the fact that there was not actually a program in
African American studies for me to direct when I was hired. My
job—in addition to teaching courses in the English department,
serving on departmental and university-wide committees, and
integrating the faculty of arts and sciences—was to create and
then run an African American Studies program, and I looked
forward to the challenge. I, like my white colleagues, believed
that because there were three Black faculty members (two
African Americans and one African) hired at the same time,
there were enough of us to make a difference. I did not question
the fact that we three, along with representing the sum total of
the African American presence in tenure-track jobs at the institution, constituted the jointly appointed core of the new program. I did not know at the time that, in its history, UMKC
had rarely employed—and never tenured—a faculty member of
African descent, and I probably would not have thought too
much about why that was the case. In short, I was thrilled when
I got the call offering me the job, and was delighted that I would
have the opportunity to shape a program, if not in my own image, at least, to my own liking. I had dreams of constructing a
program of broad intellectual vitality and interest, cutting-edge
content and methodologies, and wonderful gender balance. It
did not take long for me to realize that my understanding of
African American Studies differed, at times drastically, from that
of many of my white colleagues, and certainly from the administration's.

About five months after moving to Kansas City and starting

my new job, I had my first indication that I might be in a universe different from what I had assumed. I got myself on the agenda of the school's curriculum committee in order to propose two new literature courses I thought would be useful for both the English department and the new program in African American Studies. One course was a survey of African American literature from the Harlem Renaissance through the 1980s. The other was a course on African American women's literature. At the same time, I wanted to put the curriculum committee on notice that I would be back at the next meeting with proposals for two African American history courses.

I presented proposals along with a sample syllabus for each of the two literature courses, and I outlined how both courses would fulfill distribution requirements and be easily incorporated into the existing curriculum of the English department. When I finished my presentation, there was a very long silence, along with quite a few looks exchanged between the members of the committee. One cleared his throat and said, almost to himself, "I wonder if we aren't moving a bit too fast." I waited patiently to hear how exactly it was that the material I had presented constituted moving too fast. I was just about to ask for clarification when another committee member broke in to say, "Well, the real problem here is she seems to be suggesting that Blacks have written enough books to be taught in two separate classes. I mean, do all of you really believe that Black people wrote all the books listed here?" The meeting degenerated from there. The upshot was that I was told they would approve one of the classes, the one on Black women, because they thought Black students might like taking a class on Black women's literature from a Black woman, and besides, "Toni Morrison is certainly someone we can all agree is a really good writer."

For this group of white academics, as late as 1995, Black Studies was something far removed from a legitimate academic enterprise. It was merely to be put in place and supported as a rationale for teaching Black Students and housing Black faculty, but not for changing the institution or challenging it to change in any significant ways. Racial integration within higher education, as embodied by Black Studies, had come to be a far less radical or even guilt-producing issue for white America by the mid-1990s. However, the result placed Black people, who were often the ones doing the integrating, in a difficult position, often forcing them to inhabit an ill-defined space between white and Black communities. This was particularly true on college campuses, and African American Studies was an academic space within which those tensions came to the fore. In short, the field often came to mean very different things to white administrators and to the faculty and students charged with building and participating in such programs. To a certain extent, this had long been true.

I've recounted this, not in an effort to embarrass anyone at UMKC, or merely to vent, but because the story in many ways epitomizes the history and thinking around Black or African American Studies on numerous college campuses. I also related the incident because it illustrates the ways that Bundy's and Ford's strategy was a success yet simultaneously created a situation that continues to impact the ways that race and integration are bound up with the presence, absence, meaning, and use of African American Studies as a field. If I envisioned the program in terms of its academic and intellectual significance, the institution envisioned it as part and parcel of their two-pronged affirmative action effort to ensure a diverse faculty and student body. Where I saw an opportunity to contribute to an intellectual enterprise, the institution saw a means to solve a highly visible and racially charged problem. Attracting Black students to the institution was certainly one of the reasons the administration at UMKC gave for beginning the program at their school. However, as they began their program, they did not take into account the differences in the class makeup of the student body or the historical and social changes that had taken place in the matter of race and the academy.

Within two years I had left not only the institution, but the state of Missouri. It would take a few more years for the other two "first" hires to join me in leaving UMKC. The problem, I came to discover, was not bad luck with the institution's choice in hiring, an absence of good intentions on the part of the administrators responsible for inaugurating the program, the program's geographical location, or lack of community support. The problem was the conflicting history, various contemporary meanings, and uses of African American Studies as a field— conflicts that were unavoidable in a field designed to address any and all institutional issues involving racial inclusion and exclusion within American universities. To be sure, the often rocky terrain that is racial relationships in America has shifted since the pre–civil rights era. Yet, in many ways, African American Studies has remained static in the minds of most administrators. At the very least, there is real distance between what faculty teaching in such programs experience and the vision others hold.

I am not alone in my experience of contemporary Black Studies Programs. Nell Irvin Painter has written about the knotted relationship between Black Studies and Black faculty, "both black studies and black faculty members, often seen in countless academic minds as kindred phenomena, still face familiar frustrations." Before answering the question of what those frustrations are, Painter outlines the good news for the field and the faculty. She notes that "Black studies has experienced extraordinary intellectual growth over the span of a generation. Recent bibliographies amount to hundreds of pages, and scholars in the field produce interdisciplinary work of stunning sophistication."[20] Surely this is just the type of progress Bundy and Ford envisioned when they began deliberations about the new field. However, they probably could not have foreseen that, thirty years after the founding and institutionalization of Black Studies, a Professor at Princeton University would write that in 2000, it often seemed to her that:

> the great eraser in the sky had wiped out 30 years of progress, that we had been remanded to a version of 1969. Same dumb 1960's assumptions, same dumb 1960's questions: Even though our courses enroll masses of non-black students, even though prominent black-studies departments have had non-black leadership, and even though non-black faculty members are commonplace in black-studies departments all around the country, the presumption still holds that black studies serves only black students and employs only black faculty members. From time to time, administrators still intimate their belief that the main purpose of black studies is to forestall student dissent. And it seems that people of all racial and ethnic backgrounds can still harbor attitudes detrimental to the health of black studies. While non-black people may be more likely to ignore the field's development, a black skin does not automatically make its owner an advocate of either black studies or black faculty members. Black and non-black people can throw obstacles in the way.

She ends her look at the stagnation and changes in attitudes toward Black Studies today by saying that "in the context of American race relations, the conclusions are understandable and merit investigation by anyone interested in the health of black studies or the survival of black faculty members."[21] I would add that such conclusions and thinking merit the attention of anyone interested in race, integration, and American higher education.

Another African American professor, and a former director

of African American Studies, Gerald Early, echoes these concerns in a 2002 article:

> When I was appointed director of African-American
> studies at Washington University in St. Louis some 10
> years ago, a black friend laughingly told me I had just
> been made "the bossman of the boots." (Boots, a deroga-
> tory term for blacks, was common among us during my
> childhood.) My mother simply grunted, "Why would you
> take that job?" warning about how hard it is to work
> with other blacks and how "we like to stab each other in
> the back."

In discussing the general relationship of Black or African
American Studies to contemporary Black people, Early points
out that, unlike what was often true in the 1970s when such
programs were first institutionalized, today, "relatively few
black people, even those awed by education credentials, were
ever particularly impressed that I ran a black studies program."
Instead of pride or even curiosity, he instead heard from other
African Americans statements like, "Black people need to be
getting degrees in engineering, not black studies." In addition to
the responses he got from other African Americans, he also got
a variety of interesting responses from his white colleagues
when they heard of his directing an African American Studies
program. He goes on to say that when he:

> told white acquaintances about my job, some would be
> nonplused ("Is that a major?"), some earnest ("We need
> more diversity!"), some smirking ("What else is a black
> qualified to teach at a white school!"), some patronizing
> ("How nice for black students to have something related
> to their culture and for white students to learn something
> about it!"), some opportunistic ("Can you speak at my

church during our next black history month celebration?"), some guilt-ridden and confessional ("How horribly racist we whites are!").[22]

In describing some of the issues that faced him at Washington University in St. Louis, Early points out that there is an additional burden for Black Studies programs because, unlike any other academic unit, Black Studies programs are expected to hire only Black faculty. He notes that his colleagues feel that, while it is sometimes permissible to hire white teachers, they ultimately believe that "after all, students don't enroll in black studies to get white teachers. They can get those anywhere."[23]

Clearly, the story of my beginning the African American Studies program at UMKC is not an isolated incidence of white administrators believing that Black or African American Studies could only have one purpose or meaning. I would argue that the experiences of Painter, Early, and myself illustrate the shift in significance from the field known as Black Studies to its more contemporary manifestation as African American Studies. That difference is about more than just a name. Indeed, if at its founding, Black Studies was associated with the Black freedom struggle and Black Power, militancy, rebellion, and anger, by 1995 African American studies—while capable of evoking those types of emotions—was primarily viewed as a widely accepted and relatively benign means to integrate and desegregate institutions, faculties, and curricula. In short, it was viewed solely as an affirmative action program, although there seemed to be some confusion about who were the actual beneficiaries.

What then is the difference between a field of study organized so as to make college campuses relevant to and for students new to a white college environment and one that is designed to attract them to the institutions? Is there any real difference at all? Could it be that the meaning of race, Black Studies, and African American Studies and the nature of racial integration have remained substantially stagnant and, that as a result, the two periods of time and the two fields can be viewed in the same ways? Could it be true that conceptions of race on college campuses remained the same after the civil rights era as they had been before it? Put another way, could it be that my experience of beginning an African American Studies program at UMKC in 1995 would have been the same for someone doing so in 1968?

One of the differences between the two periods is the fact that—again, as a result of the success of the earlier strategies to create a unified meaning of and for Black Studies—the study of race in traditional disciplines is no longer quite as unusual as in earlier periods. Now, it is not only Black faculty who might be expected to put a work of fiction by an African American author on a syllabus, nor would it seem out of place for a course on American history to cover slavery or the civil rights movement, or even for a white professor to wax knowledgeable about the role of race in American culture and society. Race and Blackness was not in 1995 and is not now viewed solely as the property of Black faculty or Black Studies. However, Black Studies is still viewed by many students as the only appropriate place for Black faculty. The Ford report notes, "It is sad but true that without black studies, Chicano studies, women's studies, or Native American studies departments or programs, few colleges and universities could boast of having an integrated or pluralistic faculty."[24] To put a finer point on these findings, it would appear that the strategy that Ford developed was successful in so far as it ensured that the curricula of traditional disciplines would be integrated, but there seems to be more difficulty in ensuring that Black faculty are equally as accepted.

Still, there are internal questions in need of answering about the field and its utility for those within it, as well as questions for the colleges and universities at which the programs exist. Indeed, some have argued that while the period of institutionalization for African American studies was key, there is a need for faculty housed within the discipline as it now stands to "return to the basic question many asked in those early days, African American studies for what purpose?" While questioning, indeed arguing over, the meaning and utility of the field was integral to the early manifestation of Black studies, when faculty and students were intent on institutionalization and legitimacy, such types of dialogues are much less frequent today. In an earlier period, "Africana studies was to provide the black presence, to supply role models for students, to have an active advising and counseling function, to organize film series, lectures, and symposia, and to influence traditional departments in the composition of their faculty and curriculum."[25] Because it was so overwhelmingly viewed by college administrators in such broad terms, the role for the programs and for Black faculty associated with it was social, political, and intellectual. Admittedly, this was a great deal to ask of one field, or a handful of faculty members, especially of junior professors without tenure. Many associated with the new field found themselves exhausted and perhaps less inclined to be a part of such an endeavor. As a result of this history, today it can often be difficult to find Black faculty who are willing to have their academic appointments housed within African American Studies, thus making it even more difficult for the field to continue to flourish.

What must Bundy have thought as he watched these developments unfold? What do these circumstances tell us about his larger dream of finding innovative ways to integrate higher education through Black or African American Studies? Certainly, things did not turn out much as he had planned, and the first twenty years of the founding of African American Studies must surely have proven to him that race and racial integration are more complicated than he could have imagined. This is certainly the lesson for us today. Still, although Bundy clearly believed that he would be able to use the funds of the Ford Foundation to make a significant difference in the issue of racial tolerance, Tamar Jacoby has noted that Bundy's "writing about race changed noticeably over the years, growing if anything more concerned but also a little more melancholy, filled with an increasing sense of just how hard it is to change American hearts and minds." She notes that over the years, the certainty that marked his earlier efforts is replaced by uncertainty as "the more Bundy worked on racial matters, the clearer he saw that no social engineering could simply undo 300 years of history."[26]

Still, he never changed his fundamental convictions. He continued to believe that "the hurdles faced by African Americans were unique and therefore required unique answers."[27] Perhaps he would see the present tensions in and around African American Studies as positive developments in need of more time, money, effort, and focus to solve. Perhaps not. In 1979, in the same month that he stepped down as the president of Ford, he gave a speech in which he described his racial vision during the 1960s as naïve. He said that at the time he had "thought commitment and resources would be enough. That, if you will, was a false high, short-term reaction. The question is, do we give up. No, we believe there is still a place to attack; there are still moves you can make. If you take the longer view, you can see we have come a distance."[28]

Before Bundy stepped down as the president of the foundation, one of his most notable public opinions about race relations in higher education was his writing about the Supreme Court's *Bakke* decision. That ruling endorsed the use of racial criteria in university admissions, and Bundy's unintended contribution was an article in the *Atlantic* in 1977 that made the case for affirmative action in higher education. It was "even for Bundy, an unusually subtle and brilliant argument however... what made it important was its impact on one particular reader: Supreme Court Justice Harry Blackmun, who provided a crucial fifth vote in favor of the use of racial criteria" in the *Bakke* case.

Indeed, Blackmun's opinion was so close to Bundy's magazine article that it basically quoted him word for word. Bundy wrote in the *Atlantic* article that: "Precisely because it is not yet 'racially neutral' to be black in America, a racially neutral standard will not lead to equal opportunity." Thus, he concluded, "To get past racism, we must here take account of race."[29] Blackmun borrowed the last phrase almost verbatim, and until just a few years ago, the case and the belief that race had to be at the center of any solution to ending racial inequity in the United States was the law.

It is not surprising that McGeorge Bundy would have taken note of the case and chimed in with an opinion. The case, along with its racial thinking, was the nation's primary rationale for affirmative action in higher education, a topic long of concern to Bundy. African American Studies owes a large debt to the case; indeed, the *Bakke* decision is key for understanding the issues of race, integration, and affirmative action in higher education today.

BAKKE, AFFIRMATIVE ACTION, AND HIGHER EDUCATION, 1970–2003

Alan Bakke was a white man who was twice denied admission to a California medical school, despite having better grades and test scores than successful African American applicants. After the medical school turned him away for the second time, Bakke filed a lawsuit that set off a major controversy over the use of race in deciding admission to colleges and universities, not just medical schools. At the time, Bakke's claim was novel. He charged that he was a victim of reverse racial discrimination and argued that he had been excluded from the school because he was white. In terms of its significance to strategies for racial redress in higher education, his case is considered by many legal scholars to be the most important civil rights decision since the end of segregation.[30]

In the early 1970s, the medical school of the University of California at Davis admitted one hundred students each year and used two admissions programs and sets of criteria, one for "regular" admissions and another for "special" or minority candidates. The purpose of the special admissions program was to increase the number of minority and disadvantaged applicants and students. In the regular admissions program, applicants had to have a grade point average of at least 2.5 on a scale of 4.0, or they were automatically rejected. In the special admissions program, however, applicants could have a lower grade point average. This two-tiered system for admissions seemed to be working, as, according to court documents, from 1971 to 1974, the special program admitted twenty-one Black students, thirty Mexican Americans, and twelve Asians, for a total of sixty-three minority students. The regular program admitted one black student, six Mexican Americans, and thirty-seven Asians, for a total of forty-four minority students. No disadvantaged white candidates were admitted through the special program. This disparity was the basis for Bakke's lawsuit.

After his second rejection, he filed a lawsuit in California and asked the court to force the University of California at Davis to admit him to the medical school. He also claimed that the special admissions program violated the Fourteenth Amendment, which says in part, "No State . . . shall deny to any person . . . the equal protection of the laws." Because he was white, Bakke argued, the school was treating him unequally because of his race. The superior court agreed with Bakke and said that the special admissions program violated the federal and state constitutions and was therefore illegal.

The University of California appealed the case to the Supreme Court of California. That court also declared the special admissions policy unconstitutional and declared that Bakke had to be admitted to the medical school. The case was then appealed to the United State Supreme Court, the highest court in the land. There, while four justices confirmed that Bakke had been the victim of reverse discrimination, four others agreed that the school's affirmative action plan was a logical application of the 1964 Civil Rights Act. Justice Lewis Powell sided with both viewpoints, resulting in Bakke's admission to the school and the upholding of affirmative action.[31]

The legacy of the *Bakke* case then, was that race could be considered a plus in achieving diversity so long as it was not the only consideration. Under *Bakke,* any system of racial "set-asides" or "quotas" was unconstitutional, but some consideration could be given to race in deciding between similarly qualified applicants. That same set of considerations was again ruled upon by the Supreme Court in the summer of 2003.

On June 23, 2003, in its first ruling on affirmative action in higher education admissions in twenty-five years, the Supreme Court again ruled that race could be used in university admission decisions. But the narrowly divided court also seemed to put limits on how much of a factor race could play in giving minority students an advantage in the admissions process. The U.S. Supreme Court justices decided on two separate but parallel cases—they voted five to four to uphold the University of Michigan's law school affirmative action policy, which favors minorities, but in a six to three vote, the justices struck down the school's affirmative action policy for undergraduate admissions, which awarded twenty points for Blacks, Hispanics, and Native Americans on an admissions rating scale.

Taken together, the cases tested whether a university is allowed to discriminate because it values diversity in its student body, or whether discrimination is only justified to reverse past racial injustice. The pivotal case, *Grutter v. Bollinger,* involved the university's law school. Barbara Grutter, who is white, applied for admission there in 1996 and was rejected. She investigated and found out that African Americans and ethnic minorities who had lower overall admissions scores had been admitted. Grutter sued, claiming she was a victim of reverse discrimination, and her lawyers argued that the admissions program at the university's law school was unconstitutional. They based the argument on the *Bakke* decision.

Grutter and her supporters won the first round in U.S. District Court, but lost in a close decision in the Sixth Circuit Court of Appeals. The majority of appellate court justices sided with the university view that a diverse student body has its own benefits, and that a "points" system for admission that takes the race of the applicant into account in an overall score isn't a quota. Grutter appealed that ruling to the Supreme Court. Justice Sandra Day O'Connor was the eventual deciding vote in *Grutter*, and stated that affirmative action is still needed in America—but hoped that its days are numbered. "We expect that 25 years from now, the use of racial preferences will no longer be necessary to further the interest approved today."[32]

In relation to African American Studies, if the courts have begun to take a dim view of actual affirmative action cases, one wonders how long it will be before the powers that be begin to look closely at African American Studies as a de facto affirmative action program. What impact will an end of those programs have on the field? Even those who work in African American Studies seem to believe that this is how it most productively functions.

For example, at a 2004 conference on African American Studies on Ivy League campuses, Mary Frances Berry, chairperson of the U.S. Commission on Civil Rights, and Geraldine R. Segal, professor of American social thought and history at the University of Pennsylvania, argued that Black Studies is a viable and effective tool for social change. Professor Berry pointed out that social advancements during the last few decades, as exemplified by the increased numbers of African American faculty and students on Ivy League campuses, should be viewed as a substantive "marker of progress in education" but not "the promised land."[33] Professor Berry suggested that there was a telling connection between the growth of Black Studies programs at Ivy League institutions and the aftermath of landmark affirmative action cases such as *Brown v. Board of Education* and *Bakke v. Univ. of California*. They are, she said, indicators of "how much progress we've made in trying to open up the national life of Black people in America, without regard to race, class and other kinds of indigenous discrimination."[34]

Along those same lines, law school professor Kimberle Williams Crenshaw observed that, much as Early and Painter have argued, great strides have been made with regard to building reputable Black Studies programs that we should celebrate as markers of progress, but celebrating victories without paying attention to some of their more troubling consequences is a mistake. Many Black students, Crenshaw argued, want to cleanse themselves of the stigma of being beneficiaries of affirmative action and tend to distance themselves from the very programs that enabled their admittance. She stressed the importance of African American scholars engaging their students in discussions on the role that affirmative action and Black Studies programs have played in their success, "We haven't done a good enough job encouraging students that there is no stigma, no need to cleanse themselves," she said.[35]

Despite myriad successes between 1969 and 2005, confusion and conflict persist in a number of key areas for Black Studies or African American Studies. In addition to identity, mission, and structure—areas under debate in a majority of traditional disciplines around the country—African American studies is also engaged in an ongoing debate over whether it is a field or a discipline and about what its specific purpose might be. In all, however, by the end of the 1980s, many believed that Black Studies was very much alive as "many programs are doing well, others are experiencing difficulties, and there are miles to go before any among us will be allowed to sleep. But black studies has survived its infancy and early childhood, and it is now moving ahead into what might well be a troubled adolescence."[36]

Part of that troubled adolescence would have to include an assessment on the part of African American faculty about the very nature of the field, in light of its being viewed as little more than an affirmative action program in an era when such programs are under attack. The response of a number of programs and departments is to make themselves relevant to a wider scope of Black people.

More than just a particular nomenclature was at stake in the change from Black to African American Studies. In a very real sense, the favorable change toward the field by white administrators and the use of African American Studies to solve pressing contemporary racial issues on college campuses in the mid-1990s were a testament to the efficacy of the strategy that Bundy refined. At the same time, it was a legacy of the past, updated for use in a more contemporary period. Comparing the past use of Black Studies with the more contemporary use of African American Studies proves that racial crisis can come in myriad forms.

FROM BLACK STUDIES TO AFRICAN DIASPORA STUDIES: A SHIFT IN PERSPECTIVE

The shift in naming from Black Studies to African American studies in the late 1980s was significant. In her overview of the development of Black Studies departments and programs, which was commissioned by Ford, historian Darlene Clark Hine indicated that, while some still clung to the term "Black Studies" in the 1980s, many argued that as a designation, Black Studies was generic should be stridently opposed, given its connection with a separatist viewpoint that could be interpreted to mean that the field was only intended to be of interest to Black students and faculty. Accordingly, many institutions began in the late 1980s to show a decided preference for names such as African American Studies, African American and African World Studies, African Diaspora Studies, or Africana Studies. Each designation carries with it a particular political viewpoint and strategy, and the diversity of names speaks to the varying ways a program can position itself in relation to larger issues around race in higher education.[37] In the same way that Black Studies spoke to a more militant desire to claim power and inclusion for African Americans than did the prevailing nonviolent strategies associated with the civil rights movement, African American studies spoke most specifically to an institutionally acceptable political project divorced from and often openly contemptuous of Black Power ideologies. African Diaspora Studies embraces a Black student body that is not primarily African American and that, perhaps not surprisingly, now comprises a majority of the Black students on elite college campuses.

Those who argue for the relevancy of the term Africana or Diaspora Studies maintain that anything less "implies that the primary focus of teaching and research is the historical, cultural, and political development of Afro-Americans living within the boundaries of North America." Those who embrace the more inclusive term are arguing for more than just a specific nomenclature; they argue that to name a program or department Afro-American or African American Studies neglects those of African descent in the Caribbean and other parts of the Americas. To use the broader term, they insist, is to encompass a broader "geographical, if not disciplinary, reach, spanning both North and South America, the Caribbean, and the African continent—in short, the African Diaspora."[38] It is this focus on Caribbean and African students that forms the basis for the next chapter.

African American Studies, the field, is clearly strong enough to exhibit a "coattail effect"—long enough to assist other "studies programs" to gain institutional footing. The success of the strategies first envisioned by Bundy and the foundation has resulted in what for the 1960s and 1970s would have been unimaginable numbers of African American scholars, courses, departments, and programs, and the field serves as a model for how to "do" minority studies. At the same time, as we move into and through this next millennium, it is difficult to imagine what African American Studies will look like in the next decade. In order to adequately imagine its future, we must reassess the nature of university commitments to racial advancement, in light of the shifting nature of strategies for and obstacles to racial progress. We must also be mindful of the shifts in the enrollment numbers of African American students in colleges and universities in the United States.

6

EVERYTHING AND NOTHING AT ALL

Race, Black Studies, and
Higher Education Today

Last week, as I was leaving UC Berkeley's African-American Studies
Department at Barrows Hall, I reflected on how sad it is that so few
African Americans are seen on campus.... Over the years, the number
of blacks has dwindled nearly to embarrassing invisibility.... I had just
left a meeting with Professor Stephen Small, the new chair of the African-
American department and...what I *really* thought...was that the
department itself was partly the reason we don't have more black students
and professors at Berkeley. How could I explain...the growing schism
between the native blacks and black immigrants who control African-
American university departments across the country?
Cecil Brown[1]

African-Americans...are about to enter an identity crisis, the extent
of which we've not begun to imagine. For 200 years, the terms "race"
or "minority" connoted black-white race relations in America. All of a
sudden, these same terms connote black, white, Hispanic. Our privileged
status is about to be disrupted in profound ways.
Henry Louis Gates Jr.[2]

Despite the fact that African American academics would soon
begin to publish news of the rapidly unfolding developments on
the Internet and in the popular press, my students were the first
to alert me. In the moments before class began, or a few seconds
after it ended, I would overhear brief snatches of conversations,
dialogues that initially made little or no sense at all. "Why do we

have all these Black students and no African Americans?" Or, "He's not Black, he's Nigerian." Just bits and pieces of a narrative that I could easily have heard out of context, or misheard entirely. Slowly, over the course of a few years, my colleagues and I began to tune in to the substance of student conversations and to compare notes with each other. We would mention in passing at conferences, or over lunch, that there seemed to be fewer Black students on campus and in our classes who considered themselves to be African American, and more who identified themselves in various ways as of first- or second-generation African or Caribbean descent. "You notice that too?" was an all too frequent refrain. We were uncomfortable even making the observation, with its implicit distinctions among Black people. After all, we were talking about students who were born here in America—as the children and grandchildren of immigrants, of course—and the term "African American" seemed to describe them as succinctly as those who were not the descendants of immigrants.

Although much has changed in the forty-plus years since the integration of African American students into white universities, Black faculty today continue to notice each announcement of an increase in the minority college student population. Many of us smile widely when we hear that the numbers of Black students are climbing from 8 percent to 12 percent, then to 14 percent. Relatively small numbers overall, but a sign of progress, nonetheless. As a result, many of us are unsure about making fine-line distinctions about the ethnic background of those students. Besides, it could be considered racist, xenophobic, or, at the very least, selfish to point out that the background of our Black students seems to be shifting. Nonetheless, the conversations continue, and the Black student population continues to change. A student working on her senior thesis tracked the shrinking number of African American students at Princeton; 50 percent of Black students were the children of first- or second-generation African or Caribbean immigrants, the thesis declared.[3] "Did you get that verified by the admissions office, or some other office?" I asked, when my students told me that a young woman named Rebecca Stewart was working on the issue and mentioned her findings to them. "They don't keep track of the numbers of Black students broken down by ethnicity," was the response. That percentage would surely be stunning if true, I thought—but clearly the students had heard it wrong.

In the spring of 2004, Henry Louis Gates Jr. , Harvard University professor and director of African and African American Studies, came to Princeton and announced in a public lecture that nearly 75 percent of the Black students at Harvard College were of first- or second-generation African or Caribbean descent, or of mixed race. What those percentages mean at Harvard is that, while about 8 percent, or nearly 530 of Harvard's undergraduates are Black, close to two-thirds, or over 350 of those Black students are the children or grandchildren of either West Indian or African immigrants.[4] "We have to ask ourselves," he said to the packed audience, "where the African American students are going?" In talking with him later, it became clear that he, like I, had first heard of the specific numbers from a student. In his case, it was Aisha Haynie, who had conducted her own research a few years ago for her undergraduate thesis. Haynie said her research was "prompted by the reaction from her black classmates when she told them that she was not from the West Indies or Africa, but from the Carolinas. 'They would say, No, where are you really from?'"[5]

Finally, in June of 2004, the *New York Times* published an article on its front page entitled "Top Colleges Take More Blacks, But Which Ones?" According to those interviewed by the two reporters, Sara Rimer and Karen Arenson, admissions officers were well aware of the decrease in African American students, along with an increase in the number of Black Students, but they were unsure of how to address the issue.[6] Researchers from Princeton and the University of Pennsylvania reported that they had compiled data on the number of Black students at twenty-eight selective colleges and universities, "including theirs, as well as Yale, Columbia, Duke and the University of California at Berkeley." They found that "41 percent of the black students identified themselves as immigrants, as children of immigrants, or as mixed race."[7] Only 9 percent of Black people in America are the children of first- or second-generation immigrants, so the numbers were surprising and certainly represented a larger proportion than could be explained as the result of statistical happenstance. Later in the article, admissions officers speculated on the need for a special category of affirmative action for Blacks whose ancestry included enslavement in the United States (as opposed to the Caribbean). Further, the article noted that one Black student at Harvard whose family had been in the United States for generations said that, as a result of these demographic shifts, "there were so few black students like her at Harvard that they had taken to referring to themselves as 'the descendants'" as a way of identifying Black students who had four ancestors who had experienced enslavement in the United States.[8]

Have we really reached a point where the nineteenth-century practice of identifying Blackness as one drop of Black blood has been replaced with the requirement that all four on one's grandparents were born in the United States and descended from slaves? Is that really a marker of identity that should be embraced? If diversity is a principle we can all embrace, why should diverse groups of Black people cause such upheaval and distress? Could it really be true that Blackness could mean everything to some and, at the same time, nothing at all to others? As the reality of diversity within and between Black people comes to the fore, African American Studies finds itself again embroiled in a cultural conversation over the meaning of race and integration in higher education.

It is becoming clear that for Black students, race as constituted by both ethnicity and Blackness is shaping a modern meaning and definition of the "Negro Problem" in the twenty-first century. Undeniably, such concerns are increasingly defining the experience of Black students on college campuses. In many ways, African American Studies sits at the center of this developing controversy. Indeed, a waning concern with African Americans as a minority group has placed African American Studies in a position where the ground is constantly shifting under its institutional feet. The issue is not just an increasing number of Latinos in the United States, as referred to in this chapter's opening epigraph, but a substantial rise in the numbers of first- and second-generation students of Caribbean and African descent that has also impacted the development, utility, and organization of African American Studies as a field.

In the search for ways to integrate institutions of higher education, the focus began with efforts to address the "Negro Problem" through affirmative action and other programs aimed at correcting a past history of enslavement and disenfranchisement. Overwhelmingly, all such programs sought to increase the numbers of Black students on campuses. It has just recently occurred to administrators and scholars that there might be differences between the Black people they are attempting to recruit. However, some administrators say there is no reason to take ancestry into account when considering admission or affirmative action. For them, Black is Black, and origin is unimportant. Indeed, Lee C. Bollinger, the president of Columbia University, believes that "the issue is not origin, but social practices. It matters in American society whether you grow up black or white. It's that differential effect that really is the basis for affirmative action."[9] Although this view is clearly supported by research, for African American Studies it matters that African American students now constitute a smaller proportion of Black students.[10]

DIVERSITY IN BLACK

In 2003, the census bureau announced that the number of Latinos in the United States exceeded African Americans. There were 37 million Latinos and 36.2 million African Americans. As a *New York Times* article on these developments reported, "To some, the figures promise to shake up a field that has always relied to some extent on a political and cultural landscape that cast racial problems in black and white."[11] One scholar interviewed about the significance of these numbers for African American Studies, Kim Butler, professor of history and chair of Africana Studies at Rutgers University, noted, "We're in a new political age. A lot of the people who founded black studies programs are retired or have moved on. We do not have that political groundswell or demand to support the expansion of black studies. We're out of style."[12] Style and popularity are but some of a number of issues facing African American Studies. There are also issues with cultural memory and differences between generations of African Americans. "The clock has been turned back," says Valerie Grim, interim chairwoman of Black Studies at Indiana University at Bloomington. "The students we have today don't even know who Martin Luther King is."[13]

At its inception, Black Studies was instituted as a means of addressing and responding to the demands of increased numbers of African American students on college campuses. By the 1980s, it was viewed by administrators as a way to increase the declining African American student body on campuses. In the 1990s, it again underwent a shift in focus. In many parts of the country, "black-studies departments at public universities" began "reinventing and renaming themselves. They are changing their names to 'Africana' and 'African diaspora' studies and broadening their courses from a focus on black Americans to black people in Africa, Europe, and the Caribbean."[14] The once clear, if problematic, institutional history, mission, and utility of these programs are increasingly at odds with the contemporary needs of many colleges and universities. Indeed, since the early 1990s, many African American Studies programs have been re-structured in ways to suggest not only their embrace of the diverse intellectual project of studying Blacks in the whole of the African diaspora, but also their relevance for growing numbers of Black students and faculty of recent Caribbean and continental African descent.

In Diaspora Studies, the emphasis is not just on particular groups of Black people, but rather on the ways groups change across geographic space and time. As historian Colin Palmer, the Dodge Professor of history at Princeton University, has observed, "The interesting question is how do a people of seemingly similar background and history, placed in different contexts, produce something so different." Professor Palmer believes that the field of African American Studies should embrace a methodology more focused on the African diaspora. "We'll look at the cross-fertilization of ideas that takes place across the diaspora: Caribbean folk coming to New York, for instance, and transforming the texture of life there. Folks in the Caribbean influenced by black American traditions. This is the study of globalization, but with a particular phenotype and history."[15]

While, on the one hand, such numbers and demographic shifts ensure that there are increased numbers of Black people at schools like Harvard, on the other hand, the specific backgrounds of those students mean that "in the high-stakes world of admissions to the most selective colleges—and with it, entry into the country's inner circles of power, wealth and influence—African-American students whose families have been in America for generations" are being left behind.[16] Although it is unclear what the ultimate result of such a racial shift will be, some admissions officers and Black faculty, among others, have begun to publicly wonder about the implications of these new developments for both college campuses and the larger issues of racial equality in America as a whole. At the same time, it is clear that the widespread strategy of collapsing differences between Black people from different parts of the African diaspora also has implications for African American Studies as a field.

Indeed, while the status of African American Studies at elite colleges and universities would appear to be good (within the past few years, the University of California at Berkeley and Yale University have begun graduate programs leading to a PhD, and Harvard has begun to offer a doctorate in African and African American Studies), many programs and departments at public institutions are facing a shortage of funds, a lack of enrollment, and the necessity of reshaping their curriculum to try to attract new groups of Black people. For example, Indiana University's department of African American Studies, which has had as many as one hundred majors, only had fifty in 2005. "When you are in a program that deals with the history and culture of a particular group," says Professor Grim, "you are constantly having to reorientate with the sense of trying to be more inclusive and expand your intellectual base."[17] Three years ago, the department changed its name from Afro-American Studies to African-American and African-diaspora studies.[18] The African American Studies program at Harvard changed its name to African and African American Studies around the same time as well. At the University of Minnesota, the department's chair, Keletso E. Atkins, was clear about the relationship between a demographic shift and the field of African American Studies. In an article by Robin Wilson, printed in the *Chronicle of Higher Education,* Atkins noted that "The African population here has grown since 1990 by 620 percent. It is the fastest-growing immigrant population in the state." The article reports that Professor Atkins has tried to respond to those shifting numbers by making African American studies more welcoming to the African students on campus. She has, for instance, hired office workers from Tanzania, Ethiopia, and Somalia. One of the women, Hibaq Warsame, observed, "A lot of African Somalis don't know the black experience here. They didn't know about African-American studies."[19] Henry Louis Gates Jr. reacted to the increased attention to Black people from the wider African diaspora by noting that, "the new attention being paid to diaspora studies is in large part a ... nod to the changing demographics."[20]

Although clearly the origins of Black students is an issue that is attracting attention both within and outside of the hallowed halls of colleges and universities, some Black scholars, nonetheless, wonder if a discussion about the subject is helpful or even particularly relevant. Orlando Patterson, a Harvard sociologist who is also West Indian, wishes others would " 'let sleeping dogs lie.' The doors are wide open—as wide open as they ever will be—for native-born black middle-class kids to enter elite colleges."[21] Moreover, some within the field of African American Studies wonder if the discussion of the diverse groups of Black students on college campuses might in fact be overstated. For example, according to Professor James Turner, professor of African and African American politics and social policy at Cornell University, "We need to look critically at what's happening here. We need to ask, why is the demographic shift being proposed to us in precise terms of opposition to African Americans? And is that data accurate or is it political?"[22] His assessment is echoed by Professor Maulana Karenga, chair of Black Studies at California State University-Long Beach: "Black studies has always included Blacks of the diaspora and on the continent, and some of them were Latino, some of them were Native American, some of them were Afro-Asians. We've already done [the work in this area]; it's the European that's not reading."[23]

Cecil Brown, African American scholar and adjunct professor of English at the University of California at Berkeley, finds the trend toward a diasporic organization relevant to the future of African American Studies. Even if his concerns border on the conspiratorial, the results he describes are ultimately disturbing.

As he notes, "Putting black immigrants in leadership was part of the university's reactionary strategy to keep African Americans in line. [The department chair] wanted to offer the students more courses about the Caribbean and Africa under the aegis of 'Diaspora Studies'—code for hiring blacks from the Caribbean and Africa."[24] In any case, it is clear that the complex relationship between shifting definitions of race and Blackness and access to social mobility due to race-based initiatives has become a bone of contention for faculty within African American Studies, although there are differences in what scholars believe these numbers actually mean. As colleges and faculty members wrestle with the changing meaning of blackness, they are becoming ever more aware that this turn of events raises complex questions about race and class that have no easy answers.

If one of the roles of both African American Studies and affirmative action programs is to "correct a past injustice," then the absence in colleges and universities "of voices that are particular to being African-American, with all the historical disadvantages that that entails" should raise an alarm.[25] However, according to an article written in 2004 and printed in the *New York Times,* once a student is identified as Black, ethnicity is rarely discussed by college administrators and is considered unimportant to others in the educational field. For example, Anthony Carnevale, a former vice president at the Educational Testing Service, which develops SAT tests, said colleges were happy to the take high-performing Black students from immigrant families. "They've found an easy way out," Mr. Carnevale said. Although not commenting on what such a shift ultimately means in terms of the ability of African American students to be admitted to elite colleges, he adds, "The truth is, the higher-education community is no longer connected to the civil rights movement. These immigrants represent Horatio Alger, not Brown v. Board of Education and America's race history."[26] The children of first- or second-generation Caribbean and African immigrants are replacing those who are African American, and they are able to do so in such large numbers because, for academics and faculty, both white and Black, choosing students who are Black but disconnected from enslavement and America's history of racial injustice appears to be preferable. One Black admissions official at a selective East Coast college said the reluctance of college officials to discuss these issues "has helped obscure the scarcity of black students whose families have been in this country for generations. If somebody does not start paying attention to those who are not able to make it in, they're going to start drifting farther and farther behind."[27] As a result, not just African American students, but African American Studies may, in the not too distant future, be in increasing danger at many white colleges and universities.

The relationship of Black Studies to African American students and affirmative action, according to Edmond J. Keller, a professor of political science at the University of California at Los Angeles who teaches African American studies, is "a struggle for survival."[28] It is not so much that there is a problem with African American students today, but rather that their numbers on white college campuses have been tied up with unexplored questions of race in higher education, the utility of affirmative action programs, and the structure of African American Studies for so long that it is now difficult at times to separate them, or even notice the connection.

GETTING THERE FROM HERE:
THE FUTURE OF AFRICAN AMERICAN STUDIES

The strategy conceived and funded by Ford in the 1970s of making African American Studies an interdisciplinary program, dependent on traditional disciplines for faculty, funding, and legitimacy, is the most widely emulated model today. While certainly there are a number of full departments of African

American Studies—Harvard, Northwestern, and Temple come readily to mind—the vast majority of the over 450 academic entities on college campuses are programs. In many respects, they continue to be structured in exactly the same way as when they were first institutionalized. Since African American Studies' initial purpose was to ensure racial diversity, or more particularly, a Black presence on campuses and Black texts on college syllabi, the structure of most programs was substantially connected to traditional disciplines. The Ford Foundation went to great lengths to create the most productive organizational strategy and most often settled on a program model as the one to support, and most importantly, fund. As Nathan Huggins noted, "The models on which Afro-American studies programs were built were influenced by ideology and conditions on individual campuses...each particular form had intrinsic strengths and weaknesses."[29] In some instances, those weaknesses substantially outweigh the strengths, and certainly, they bear a relationship to contemporary understanding and discussions of race on college campuses.

Once colleges and universities began to approve requests for Black Studies departments and programs, the reality of what such a field would mean for institutions, professors, community members, and students became a topic of heated and often troubling debate. Significantly, the struggle over how the new field would be implemented, framed, financed, and institutionalized pitted luminaries from the civil rights movement against those in the newly burgeoning Black Power movement. This confrontation emphasized the stresses and strains between those who advocated integration as a sole solution to African American disenfranchisement and exclusion, and those who advocated a strategy of Black militancy as the fastest road to racial equality. The staging ground for this confrontation was centered on and within America's colleges and universities. The options, according to many, were in terms of either racial integration or Black separatism.

The contemporary manifestation of dialogues and beliefs about how race and ethnicity are understood and played out on college campuses is not disconnected from the presence, development, and organization of African American Studies. Indeed, the story of the changes in the composition of the Black student body is the latest chapter in a much longer story of African American Studies and the crisis of race in higher education. Today, as a result of a shift in racial demographics in the United States, and an exponentially more complicated dialogue over race and diversity in higher education, African American Studies as a field is embarking on an increasingly difficult search for institutional utility, meaning, and purpose. In the 1970s, when discussions of "race" were understood in our collective cultural lexicon to either rightly or wrongly refer to relationships between Blacks and whites, African American Studies was thought to be an avenue leading toward more harmonious racial relationships between those two groups. Today, in addition to offering a paradigm for understanding larger discussions around diversity, the field is also central to the shifting realities of diversity among Black people in the United States.

Toward that end, when someone recently asked me to explain why I thought that the student protest that led to the creation of African American Studies was a story worth telling, I realized that the answer had as much to do with me, or more accurately with my personal interest in the past and its connection to the future, as it did with my desire to craft a narrative history for others to read and critique. Indeed, the personal memories I conjure from what was the height of the Black Power or nationalist movement in the United States are closely tied to larger collective imaginings and narratives about the founding of Black Studies that have been, to use a phrase from Morrison's *Beloved,* "disremembered." I wonder if it is possible that the absence of a historical narrative engaging the founding of the field is best explained as an act of willful forgetting.

I am drawn to this particular moment in time and the events

that played themselves out during the founding days of African American Studies not solely because it is tied to my work in an African American Studies program. As is often true with memory, both cultural and personal, the moments I summon form a tapestry that acts as a backdrop and helps to explain the more public and academic reasons why I am interested in thinking and writing about African Americans during specific periods of time. Quite simply, I believe there is a story here in need of passing on. I believe we have memories, personal and shared, large and small, that are in need of context and explanation. I believe that re-memory is as much a choice as is forgetting. As a result, although often lacking in institutional stability and security, these programs are ground zero for broad-based discussions about the shifting nature, makeup, and meaning of race, diversity, integration, and desegregation in the United States. They also point to the declining presence and significance of African Americans in institutions of higher learning. Few recognize or acknowledge that this is the case, and no works have attempted to look at the role African American Studies has played in these developments. Nowhere is this more true than in contemporary discussions of racial specificity and difference, which drive our present understanding of our culture and our time. Mostly, I know that people are complex, history is incomplete, and memories can form the basis for larger, collective conversations.

One of those conversations should focus on race, and African American Studies as a field can provide a paradigm for doing just that. This is particularly true within the context of dialogues seeking to replace discussions about racially specific programs for social progress with colorblind notions of diversity. Indeed, the increasing focus on diversity in higher education has produced a multitude of paradigms and circumstances around the question of race that complicate earlier understandings of what it meant and why it mattered. The ways that we as a country have come to talk—or more particularly, create strategies for not talking—about race directly can often produce immature moments of interaction. Given the difficulty of understanding why differences among Black people matter, maturity is clearly called for. Within this context, racial diversity, as a popular term, is both a savior and a curse. At the same time, it shapes the ways many in such institutions come to think about race.

While the differences among Black people from the Caribbean, Africa, and the United States might seem to be small, this demographic shift has had an impact on the ability of African Americans to enroll in elite colleges and universities, and on the shape of African American Studies on college campuses. As a graduate student at the University of Minnesota, Wynfred Russell, has pointed out, "The African immigrants are the new group in town, and everyone is embracing them at the expense of black students."[30] To be sure, the subtext for the concerns about ethnic diversity within and among Black people is the shift in affirmative action efforts away from a desire to promote racial justice specifically for African Americans, and toward the amorphous benefits of "racial diversity" on campuses.

PROFILES IN DIVERSITY IN HIGHER EDUCATION, OR, WHAT'S RACE GOT TO DO WITH IT?

On a majority of college campuses, the freshman orientation week activities feature a workshop, forum, or lecture on racial diversity. Unlike earlier decades when colleges and universities may or may not have embraced racial difference, today most institutions make an effort to ensure that both minority students and others know what is expected of them in terms of racial tolerance. They celebrate the many different kinds of students who will make up the classes in the upcoming years. Orientation week is hectic, full of speeches, reflections, anecdotes, and advice. The session on diversity, at least on my own campus, is described as a day the organizers hope will be memorable. They hope it will be a symbol for the need to reflect on diversity in all its guises and to try to make sense of what diversity and difference really mean in our cultural consciousness and daily lives. The students are told that differences are not inherently bad and that diversity does not have to result in conflict. It is conceivable that the students will find themselves struggling with the difficulties of difference and diversity, perhaps most forcefully when they are not expecting to.

Although diversity is lived and experienced on college campuses in a multitude of ways, I want to explore racial diversity and share a few stories about racial interaction on Princeton's campus. The stories do point to the necessity for intelligent discussions that do more than just celebrate diversity, but instead explore the complexities of race in the United States. It is within this context that African American Studies shapes the contours of our ability to think in complex ways about race. This is true if we are thinking and talking about whites or about Blacks, Asians, or any of the other groups not considered dominant within the United States. As Dwight Brooks, the chair of African American Studies at Northwestern University, has written, "The reason that race, gender, class, and sexuality can be taken as seriously as they are and be as central to how we now produce knowledge even in traditional disciplines is a direct result of the intellectual and institutional work that has for so long proceeded at the margins of the academy in departments like African American studies."[31]

One of the things students learn about race at Princeton is that race is a social construction. They learn that there is no biological basis for racial classifications. They learn that it is society and culture (not science) that make distinctions of good, better, best based solely on racial affiliations. Most students arrive at college knowing that all people and groups are equal and that diversity and difference should be celebrated. However, an exchange from 2003 over race and medicine makes me wonder what is at stake in our view of racial diversity as a minor difference. The issue involved an exchange in the *New England Journal of Medicine* that was written about in the *New York Times*.[32] On one side, a group of doctors maintained that race had no scientific basis and should not be a consideration for doctors when prescribing medicine. Conversely, another group of doctors indicated that some medicines appeared to act differently in different racial groups. The fact that certain medications for heart disease, for example, were consistently less effective in African Americans than they were in those of European ancestry was an issue that the second group of doctors believed should be further explored. They also wanted to examine why certain cancer drugs performed differently in people with different racial ancestry.[33]

In response to the finding of a medical basis for racial difference, the first group of doctors claimed that, while the results needed to be investigated, race could not possibly be the cause for the different responses to the drugs, given that race is socially constructed. The second group acknowledged that the first group was probably right, but proposed that there might be instances when biological racial differences exist and could help to more effectively treat people who belong to certain racial groups. The question that this exchange raised for me had to do with the possibility that our desire to view all racial groups as equal and, therefore the same, might be putting lives at risk. When we insist on racial diversity as an opportunity to celebrate difference, could there be more at stake than a moment of cultural harmony? Could this particular rhetoric blind us to very real racial differences that, instead of celebration, are in need of exploration and study?

My reflection on racial diversity in a university setting is based on three stories, or moments, that raise questions about racial diversity for which I do not have answers. One involves an interaction between Asian and Asian American students; one concerns interactions between white and African American students; and the last is about African American students interacting with each other. They pose a series of questions about how the construct of racial diversity, coupled with a limited understanding of race, can cause conflict despite our best intentions. These stories ask us to think about how the world of popular culture, as well as daily interaction, might hold lessons as important as those found in books and articles.

STORY #1:

A few years ago, in the spring of 2002, the clothiers Abercrombie and Fitch briefly inaugurated a t-shirt line featuring caricatures of Asian Americans. The characters pictured on the t-shirts all had curved slits for eyes, large heads, and small bodies. The slogans on the t-shirts said things like "Wong Brothers Laundry Service: Two Wongs can make it white" and "Pizza Dojo: Eat in or Wok out. You Love Long Time." Drawing on both visual and cultural stereotypes of Asians, these t-shirts were, according to a spokesperson for the company, manufactured in good fun. "We personally thought Asians would love this T-shirt," said a spokesperson for the company.[34] Leaving aside the question of why Abercrombie and Fitch assumed that there would be a market for such images—as well as the fact that the t-shirts became collectible items on e-Bay, commanding prices three to four times what they sold for in the store—I want to focus on the response to the t-shirts by students on Princeton's campus.

The Asian Pacific Heritage Month committee joined with other groups around the country to undertake an immediate campaign to have the t-shirts pulled from circulation. Their efforts included petitions and a call-in campaign to the Abercrombie and Fitch customer service line. The committee also publicized the existence of the t-shirts on their Web site and organized a meeting to discuss the issue. Two of the students involved in raising awareness of the issue on campus were taking classes with me that semester, and during office hours we discussed their efforts. The response that bewildered both students came from Asians who thought the t-shirts were humorous, not particularly racially biased, and that the issue itself was being blown out of proportion. There is a Yoruba saying that goes, "It's not what you call me, it's what I answer to." For a handful of Asian and Asian American students, calling on racial stereotypes to describe them made far less difference than whether or not they chose to answer. The questions for my students became: Is consensus a necessary prerequisite for deeming racism either present or absent, and what does it mean if the intended target of a racially based action doesn't care?

STORY #2:

Every few years I teach a course entitled "Migration, Urban Space and African American Culture." The point of the course is to look at how changes in migration patterns for African Americans, from rural to urban and suburban areas, have influenced how we view African American culture. To put it another way, the course explored what geographic space has to do with views of race. For one assignment, the class watched two episodes of an HBO miniseries called *The Corner*. This miniseries, with an African American director, was based on a book by the same white author whose work became the basis for the long-running television series entitled *Homicide: Life on the Street*. *The Corner* chronicles the lives of a handful of people who either used or sold crack in inner-city Baltimore during the course of one month.

The characters, based on real people, would at first glance be familiar as stereotypical caricatures of African Americans. In one household, the mother is so focused on buying crack that she often forgets to shop for food, make sure her children get to school, or attend teacher conferences and school events. She shoplifts from suburban shopping centers when she needs gifts to celebrate her nine-year-old son's birthday or money to pay the utilities. Her sister, who also lives in the house and is also an addict, regularly takes the rent money and spends it on the corner. Another household features a grown son who breaks his parents' hearts repeatedly by stealing from them in order to buy crack and heroin. There is a social worker fighting an uphill battle to keep her recreation center open, in the hopes of providing positive and constructive activities for the young children at risk in a world overwhelmed by drugs. There are numerous characters, all familiar, all hopeless, and all making problematic choices and living desperate lives.

Two responses from the class discussion have stayed with me. The response of many of the African American students was that these characters were an embarrassment. There was nothing about any of their lives that was positive or uplifting, and the students did not believe that these stories were based on real life, as "black people just don't really act like that." The response from one of the white students in particular was equally dismissive of the program. She said simply that the show frustrated her because "there is no one for me to feel sorry for and besides, I don't like any of them. When you see people like this, there is always supposed to be someone you like and feel sorry for." All agreed that the program was flawed. All agreed that this was primarily because what they saw made them uncomfortable. All agreed that their comfort was a prerequisite for success. The question is: Is a clear victim, loser, or sympathetic character necessary to advance a successful argument about racial inequity? That is, do we have to like, understand, or be moved to pity a group, for a representation of race to be considered as "real"?

STORY #3:

The last story is based on the senior thesis of a student, Audrey Davis, who graduated from Princeton in 2002.[35] Theses are generally original pieces of research that allow students to explore an area of culture or scholarship, and represent a culmination of what they have learned. Davis was a psychology major, who was also getting a certificate in African American Studies, and she chose to study the racial climate on campus for African Americans. However, instead of only focusing on how African American students on campus felt in relation to white students and teachers, she broadened her questions to ask how intraracial interactions affected the psychological health of African American students. She completed her research by surveying 94 percent of the African American students on campus at the time (6 percent chose for various reasons not to participate) and came up with survey questions asking those students to rank their sense of isolation and alienation in response to various factors.

What she found was that, overwhelmingly, the feelings of depression, isolation, and hopelessness increased with the distance from groups of African American students. She further found that such isolation was often perceived as having been consciously inflicted, as a result of a number of factors. For example, if some African American students chose to dress or talk in ways that were not perceived as "keepin' it real," they could be banished from the group. If individual African American students were believed to be more interested in spending time with friends who were not African American, they could again be banished from the group. If some students were less than quick to acknowledge other African American students when they met on campus, or were not assiduous in their attendance at social and political events held by African American groups on campus, they could be banished from the group. What this student found was that the pressure of *being* African American in cer-

tain ways or of *performing* their race in ways deemed appropriate by the group exacerbated the pressure students felt coming
from outside. The questions are: Who decides what is an appropriate racial performance, where it is it learned, and how is it
that such performances are so clearly recognized?

These stories are, for me, extremely thought provoking. Does it
matter whether or not some believe that responding to instances
of racial stereotyping is still of primary concern? Is it possible
to advance the cause of racial tolerance and understanding if the
characters charged with doing the advancing are disliked? Why
are certain forms of being, looking, dressing, and acting still so
firmly tied with views of race? If I have a moral, it is that race
isn't understood in neat easy lessons or talks about diversity, and
if there is a warning, it is that race is a profoundly complicated
construct. Students need ways to theorize about race, because
there are feelings, circumstances, and moments that catch us all
unaware and run counter to what we think that we know and
believe. What we read, what we wear, what we watch on television, whom we choose to speak with can all be pertinent moments in which to better understand race.

African American Studies has already both asked the questions and posited responses. It offers ways to theorize about
race, instead of just discuss it. There are however, still questions
needing answers, and connections to be made. There are ways
of seeing that ask us to go beyond the simple need to be aware,
treat others as we would like to be treated, and have tolerance.
The key to the answers is the willingness to ask the questions. In
many ways, the question of what it means that there is diversity
among Black people is one for which many institutions still do
not have an answer. Indeed, many in higher education are unaware that this significant question must be posed. In our contemporary, post–civil rights, postmodern era, discussions about

race and racial justice and injustice have become dialogues featuring the oft-used buzzword "diversity," and racial diversity is made up of an ever-increasing number of groups. At the same time, pointing to and focusing on racial difference has become an un-American activity to be avoided at all costs. As a result, the passage of time and changing cultural circumstances have made it all the more difficult for African American Studies to make the argument that the field should remain focused squarely on Blackness in general and/or on African Americans in particular. Still, America needs African American Studies now more than ever before.

Because "race" in American culture is no longer strictly defined as Black, and Black no longer exclusively means African American, the field has been forced to shift its strategies and self-concept in order to grow and survive. Those shifts directly relate to changes in America's social interest in and strategies for acknowledging and addressing race, racism, and integration on college campuses. Few recognize, know, or acknowledge that African American Studies is central to all of these concerns, and, to my knowledge, no works have attempted to look at the role African American Studies has played in these troubling developments. Paradoxically, African American Studies as a field stands at what has become a crowded racial and political intersection. The question at the heart of *White Money/Black Power* is whether it will cross safely to the other side, or be run over while we gaze inattentively in another direction.

ACKNOWLEDGMENTS

As is so often true when given the opportunity to publicly thank those who help me in ways both large and small, I had a hard time knowing how best to do so and not write another book in the process. There are, however, a number of people who were key in this process. It is a pleasure to be able to thank them.

To Gertrude Frazier, a former program officer at the Ford Foundation, for giving me the opportunity to think about the relationship between philanthropic organizations and the development of African American Studies. Thank You.

To the Program in African American Studies at Princeton University, for understanding the need for missed days, wandering focus, and rambling conversation. Thank You.

To Gayatri Patnaik, my editor at Beacon Press, for patience, a fast turnaround time, and a scary ability to understand what I meant to say even when the words on the page would have suggested otherwise. Thank You.

To Jean Wiley, my "auntie" and editor, for helping me work through the rough spots, reminding me what was important about the Black student protest movement, and smoothing out my thinking and writing. Thank You.

To Daphne Brooks, my friend and colleague, for reading all those drafts, asking all those questions, taking this project seriously, and always encouraging me to do more. Thank You.

To Bill Gaskins, my husband and friend, for the encouragement, for the faith, and for the ever constant commitment to my health and sanity. Thank You.

NOTES

1. WHITE MONEY/BLACK POWER: THE FORD FOUNDATION AND BLACK STUDIES

1. In 1969, Jerry Farber published a book entitled *The Student as Nigger*, which argued that all students, regardless of color, were viewed and treated as "niggers" by the large corporate interests running the country and the war in Vietnam. He drew particular parallels between the Watts riot in 1965 and the student protest movement. It is probable that the singer referenced in this chapter's epigraph is familiar with this work, as Farber did quite a bit of lecturing on college campuses on this topic in advance of publishing his book. See Jerry Farber, *The Student as Nigger: Essays and Stories* (New York: Pocket Books, 1970).

2. Stephen Alan Jones, "The Revolution Will Not Be Televised: Black Studies and the Transformation of American Higher Education, 1967–1972" (unpublished dissertation, Michigan State University, 2003) 4.

3. Nell Irvin Painter, "Black Studies, Black Professors, and the Struggles of Perception," *The Chronicle of Higher Education*, December 15, 2000.

4. "Black Studies Is an Unpopular Major," *The Journal of Blacks in Higher Education* (2003).

5. Ibid.

6. Ibid.

7. Nathan I. Huggins, *Afro-American Studies: A Report to the Ford Foundation* (New York: Ford Foundation, 1985) 6.

8. Ibid.

9. Huggins, *Afro-American Studies*, 7.

10. Ibid.

11. Huggins, *Afro-American Studies*, 8.

12. C. H. Arce, "Historical, Institutional, and Contextual Determi-

nants of Black Enrollment" (unpublished dissertation, University of Michigan, 1976); Huggins, *Afro-American Studies;* Thomas, ed., *Black Students in Higher Education.*

13. May 4th Task Force, "The Berkeley Invention Expands" (Kent State, 2005), available online at http://dept.kent.edu/may4/ Campus_Unrest/campus_unrest_chapter1d.htm.

14. Ibid.

15. Ibid.

16. Huggins, *Afro-American Studies,* 9.

17. Ibid.

18. Huggins, *Afro-American Studies,* 21.

19. Huggins, *Afro-American Studies,* 41–42.

20. Jones, "The Revolution Will Not Be Televised," 19.

21. Eldridge Cleaver, "Education and the Revolution," *The Black Scholar* 1, no. 2 (1969): 51.

22. Robinson et al., *Black Studies in the University,* 37.

23. Fabio Rojas, "Organizational Decision Making and the Emergence of Academic Disciplines" (unpublished dissertation, Harvard University, 2002) 72.

24. Tamar Jacoby, "McGeorge Bundy: How the Establishment's Man Tackled America's Problem with Race," *Alicia Patterson Foundation Magazine* (1991).

2. BY ANY MEANS NECESSARY: STUDENT PROTEST AND THE BIRTH OF BLACK STUDIES

1. "List of Student Demands," in San Francisco State College Strike Collection (Special Collections/Archives, J. Paul Leonard Library, San Francisco State University).

2. Ibid.

3. Ibid.

4. William H. Orrick, *Shut It Down! A College in Crisis: San Francisco State College, October 1968–April 1969. A Report to the National Commission on the Causes and Prevention of Violence* (Washington, D.C.: U.S. Government Printing Office, 1969) 1.

5. Ibid.

6. Orrick, *Shut It Down!,* 2

7. Orrick, 4.

8. "List of Student Demands," San Francisco State College Strike Collection.

9. Orrick, *Shut It Down!*, 29.

10. Orrick, 4.

11. Orrick, 5.

12. Ibid.

13. "Port Huron Statement," available online at: lists.village.virginia .edu/sixties/HTML_docs/Resources/Primary/Manifestos/SDS_ Port_Huron.html.

14. Ibid.

15. Ibid.

16. Ibid.

17. Mario Savio, "Mario Savio's Speech before the Free Speech Movement Sit-In" (1964), available from The Free Speech Movement Archives Home Page, http://www.fsm-a.org/stacks/mario/mario_ speech.html.

18. Ibid.

19. "Port Huron Statement."

20. *The Columbia Revolt* (San Francisco: California Newsreel, 1968).

21. Lawrence E. Davies, "College Head Quits, Criticizing Reagan," *New York Times*, February 23, 1986.

22. John Summerskill, *President Seven* (New York: World Publishing Company, 1971) 5.

23. Orrick, *Shut It Down!*, 20–21.

24. Summerskill, *President Seven*, 132.

25. Orrick, *Shut It Down!*, 113.

26. Ibid.

27. *Daily Gater*, November 6, 1967, 1.

28. Orrick, *Shut It Down!*, 34.

29. Orrick, 114.

30. Orrick, 113.

31. Summerskill, *President Seven*, 24.

32. "Militants' Invasion Paralyzes Campus," *New York Times*, November 7, 1968.

33. Ibid.

34. Ibid.

35. Orrick, *Shut It Down!*, 133.

36. Orrick, 114.

37. Orrick, 135.

38. Orrick, 34.

39. Orrick, 104.

40. Ibid.

41. Orrick, 105.

42. Ibid.

43. Wallace Turner, "Classes Resume after Protest at College on Coast," *New York Times,* December 3, 1968.

44. Wallace Turner, "Police Repel Students at College in San Francisco," *New York Times,* December 4, 1968.

45. Turner, "Classes Resume after Protest at College on Coast," 29.

46. Turner, "Police Repel Students at College in San Francisco."

47. Nathan I. Huggins, *Afro-American Studies: A Report to the Ford Foundation* (New York: Ford Foundation, 1985) 82.

48. Caleb Rossiter, "Cornell's Student Revolt of 1969: A Rare Case of Democracy on Campus," *The Progressive* (May 5, 1999): 6.

49. Downs, *Cornell '69: Liberalism and the Crisis of the American University,* vii.

50. Downs, *Cornell '69,* 9.

3. NATION BUILDING IN THE BELLY OF THE BEAST

1. McGeorge Bundy, "A Note from the Director," *Ford Foundation Annual Report* (1967) 2.

2. Tamar Jacoby, "McGeorge Bundy: How the Establishment's Man Tackled America's Problem with Race," *Alicia Patterson Foundation Magazine* (1991); "McGeorge Bundy," *New York Times,* August 3, 1966.

3. "McGeorge Bundy," 7.

4. Ibid.

5. Bundy, "A Note from the Director," 4.

6. "McGeorge Bundy," 3.

7. Roger Wilkins, "Inter-Office Memorandum from Roger Wilkins to McGeorge Bundy Re: Afro-American Studies," May 22, 1969, Ford Foundation Archives, Office Papers of McGeorge Bundy, Box 1, Folder 5.

8. Jacoby, "McGeorge Bundy: How the Establishment's Man Tackled America's Problem with Race."

9. Bundy, "A Note from the Director," 4.

10. Nathaniel Norment Jr., *The African American Studies Reader* (Durham, North Carolina: Carolina Academic Press, 2001) vi.

11. Fabio Rojas, "Organizational Decision Making and the Emergence of Academic Disciplines" (unpublished dissertation, Harvard University, 2002) 45–46.

12. Wilkins, "Inter-Office Memorandum."

13. Norment, *The African American Studies Reader,* xxii.

14. Kenneth B. Clark, "Letter of Resignation from Board of Directors of Antioch College," in A. Philip Randolph, ed., *Black Studies: Myths & Realities* (New York: A. Philip Randolph Educational Fund, 1969) 33.

15. Bayard Rustin, "Introduction," in A. Philip Randolph, ed., *Black Studies: Myths & Realities* (New York: A. Philip Randolph Educational Fund, 1969) 3.

16. Ibid.

17. Norment, *The African American Studies Reader*, xiii.

18. Manning Marable, *Dispatches from the Ebony Tower: Intellectuals Confront the African American Experience* (New York: Columbia University Press, 2000) 5.

19. St. Clair Drake, lecture at Brooklyn College, September 23, 1969, cited in Ronald Bailey, "Black Studies in Historical Perspective," *Journal of Social Issues* 29, no. 1 (1973): 298.

20. Arthur L. Smith, "The Emergence of Black Studies," Afro-American Studies Position Papers, 17 (Los Angeles: UCLA, Center for Afro-American Studies, 1973).

21. Stephen Alan Jones, "The Revolution Will Not Be Televised: Black Studies and the Transformation of American Higher Education, 1967–1972" (unpublished dissertation, Michigan State University, 2003) 28.

22. Armstead L. Robinson et al., *Black Studies in the University: A Symposium* (New Haven: Yale University Press, 1969) vii.

23. Ibid.

24. Ibid.

25. Robinson et al., *Black Studies in the University,* 7.

26. Robinson et al., 13.

27. Robinson et al., 17.

28. Robinson et al., 169.

29. Ibid.

30. Robinson et al., *Black Studies in the University,* 172.

31. Robinson et al., 39.

32. Robinson et al., 172.

33. Kai Bird, *The Color of Truth: McGeorge Bundy and William Bundy, Brothers in Arms: A Biography* (New York: Simon & Schuster, 1998) 15–16.

34. The Bay of Pigs invasion was an unsuccessful attempt by United States–backed Cuban exiles to overthrow the government of Fidel Castro. By the time the fighting ended on April 19, 1961, ninety exiles had been killed, and the rest had been taken prisoner. The Cuban missile crisis was a tense Cold War confrontation between the United States and the Soviet Union that brought the two nations dangerously close to nuclear war in October 1962.

35. James Baldwin, *The Fire Next Time* (New York: Modern Library, 1963) 8.

36. Frantz Fanon, *The Wretched of the Earth*, Constance Farrington, trans. (New York: Grove Press, 1968) 42.

37. G. Louis Heath and the Black Panther Party, *Off the pigs! The History and Literature of the Black Panther Party* (Metuchen, New Jersey: Scarecrow Press, 1976) 4.

38. Bundy, "A Note From the Director," 4.

39. Jacoby, "McGeorge Bundy: How the Establishment's Man Tackled America's Problem with Race."

40. Ibid.

41. Ibid.

42. Lawrence Stern and Richard Harwood, "Ford Foundation: Its Works Spark Backlash," *Washington Post*, November 2, 1969.

43. Jacoby, "McGeorge Bundy: How the Establishment's Man Tackled America's Problem with Race."

44. Ibid.

45. Roldo Bartimole, "Ralph Locher: A Dose of 1960s History, or, Why Cleveland Mayors are Expendable" (2004), available online at http://www.lakewoodbuzz.com/RoldoBartimole/RB-08-09-04-Locher.html.

46. Ibid.

47. Ibid.

48. Ibid.

49. Ibid.

50. Joseph C. Goulden, *The Money Givers* (New York: Random House, 1971) 24.

51. Ibid.

52. Ibid.

53. Carl B. Stokes, *Promises of Power: A Political Autobiography* (New York: Random House, 1971) 97.
54. Bartimole, "Ralph Locher: A Dose of 1960s History, or, Why Cleveland Mayors are Expendable."
55. Bird, *The Color of Truth*, 381.
56. Jacoby, "McGeorge Bundy: How the Establishment's Man Tackled America's Problem with Race."
57. Ibid.
58. Bird, *The Color of Truth*, 381.
59. Jerald E. Podair, *The Strike That Changed New York: Blacks, Whites, and the Ocean Hill-Brownsville Crisis* (New Haven: Yale University Press, 2002) 125.
60. Jacoby, "McGeorge Bundy: How the Establishment's Man Tackled America's Problem with Race."
61. Ibid.
62. Podair, *The Strike That Changed New York*, 117.
63. Podair, 212
64. Podair, 114.
65. Goulden, *The Money Givers*, 79.

4. BLACK STUDIES IN WHITE AND BLACK: THE FORD FOUNDATION FUNDS BLACK STUDIES

1. Roger Wilkins, "Inter-Office Memorandum from Roger Wilkins to McGeorge Bundy Re: Afro-American Studies," May 22, 1969, Ford Foundation Archives, Office Papers of McGeorge Bundy, Box 1, Folder 5.
2. McGeorge Bundy, "A Note from the Director," in *Ford Foundation Annual Report* (1967) 4.
3. Wilkins, "Inter-Office Memorandum."
4. Ibid.
5. W. Arthur Lewis, "Untitled Letter to McGeorge Bundy," 1969 (Office Papers of McGeorge Bundy, Ford Foundation Archives).
6. Ibid.
7. Ibid.
8. Wilkins, "Inter-Office Memorandum."
9. Ibid.
10. Ibid.
11. Ibid.

12. James W. Armsey, "Interoffice Memorandum: On Black Studies," 1969 (Ford Foundation Archives).

13. Ibid.

14. James J. Scanlon, "Where the Rocks Are Likely to Come From," May 21, 1969 (Ford Foundation Archives).

15. Scanlon, "Where the Rocks Are Likely to Come From."

16. Nathan Hare, "Questions and Answers About Black Studies," in *African American Studies Reader*, ed. Nathaniel Norment Jr. (Durham, North Carolina: North Carolina Academic Press, 2001) 88.

17. Mary Waalkes, "A Matter of Perspective," a review of Eric A. Anderson and Alfred A. Moss Jr.'s *Dangerous Donations: Northern Philanthropy and Southern Black Education, 1902–1930*, available at http://www.h-net.org/reviews/showrev.cgi?path=23922969 481222 (H-South, September, 2000).

18. Ibid.

19. Ibid.

20. Eric Anderson and Alfred A. Moss, *Dangerous Donations: Northern Philanthropy and Southern Black Education, 1902–1930* (Columbia, Missouri: University of Missouri Press, 1999) 122.

21. James Anderson, *The Education of Blacks in the South, 1860–1935* (Chapel Hill, North Carolina: University of North Carolina Press, 1988) 39; and Raymond Wolters, *The New Negro on Campus: Black College Rebellions of the 1920s* (Princeton, New Jersey: Princeton University Press, 1975) 192.

22. Rojas, "Organizational Decision Making and the Emergence of Academic Disciplines," 85–88.

23. Wilkins, "Inter-Office Memorandum."

24. Walter Fisher, "Memorandum to John Scanlon Re: The Morgan State Negro Studies Syllabus Project," November 8, 1972 (Ford Foundation Archives).

25. James J. Scanlon, "Interoffice Memorandum to the Files: Afro-American Studies at Morgan State College," March 21, 1969 (Ford Foundation Archives).

26. Rojas, "Organizational Decision Making and the Emergence of Academic Disciplines," 81.

27. Wilkins, "Inter-Office Memorandum."

28. Harold Howe, Untitled Interoffice Memorandum to McGeorge Bundy," 1972 (Ford Foundation Archives).

29. Charles E. Izzard, "Letter to John Scanlon," 1969 (Ford Foundation Archives).

30. Elton Hinshaw, "Letter to Marion Coolen," 1971 (Ford Foundation Archives).

31. Akbar Muhammad, "Letter to Dean Wendell G. Holladay," 1971 (Ford Foundation Archives) 1.

32. Muhammad, "Letter to Dean Wendell G. Holladay," 2.

33. Ibid.

34. Elias Blake and Henry Cobb for the Task Force Group for Survey of Afro-American Studies Programs, *Black Studies: Issues in Their Institutional Survival* (Washington, D.C.: U.S. Department of Health, Education, and Welfare, Office of Education, 1976) iii.

35. Blake and Cobb, *Black Studies: Issues in Their Institutional Survival*, 29.

36. Robert Allen, "Politics of the Attack on Black Studies," *Black Scholar* 6 (September 1974): 2, 5.

37. Rojas, "Organizational Decision Making and the Emergence of Academic Disciplines," 81.

38. Irwin Ross, "McGeorge Bundy and the New Foundation Style," *Fortune* (April 1968).

39. Bundy, "A Note from the Director," 3.

40. Stephen Alan Jones, "The Revolution Will Not Be Televised: Black Studies and the Transformation of American Higher Education, 1967–1972" (unpublished dissertation, Michigan State University, 2003) 7.

41. Jones, 5.

42. Jones, 6.

43. Alice O'Connor, "The Ford Foundation and Philanthropic Activism in the 1960s," in *Philanthropic Foundations: New Scholarship, New Possibilities*, Ellen C. Lagemann, ed. (Bloomington, Indiana: Indiana University Press, 1999) 116.

44. Gerald Early, "Black Studies: The Good and the Bad," *New York Times*, April 14, 2002.

5. THE LEGACY IN THE PRESENT

1. Gerald Early, "Black Studies: The Good and the Bad," *New York Times*, April 14, 2002.

2. Robert S. Boynton, "The New Intellectuals," *Atlantic Monthly* (March 1995).

3. Ibid.

4. Nell Irvin Painter, "Black Studies, Black Professors, and the Struggles of Perception," *The Chronicle of Higher Education*, December, 15, 2000.

5. Ibid.

6. Thomas Sowell, *Affirmative Action around the World: An Empirical Study* (New Haven: Yale University Press, 2004) 175.

7. Sowell, 164.

8. Robert L. Harris, Darlene Clark Hine, and Nellie Y. McKay, *Black Studies in the United States: Three Essays* (New York: Ford Foundation, 1990).

9. Ibid.

10. Henry Louis Gates Jr., "African American Studies in the 21st Century," *The Black Scholar* (2001): 29.

11. "Black Studies Is an Unpopular Major," *The Journal of Blacks in Higher Education* (2003): 1.

12. Nikhil Pal Singh, *Black Is a Country: Race and the Unfinished Struggle for Democracy* (Cambridge, Massachusetts: Harvard University Press, 2004) 10.

13. Harris, Hine, and McKay, *Black Studies in the United States: Three Essays*.

14. James J. Scanlon, "Inter-Office Memorandum to the Files: Seminar on Afro-American Studies Aspen, Colorado," July 19–24, 1971 (Ford Foundation Archives).

15. Nathan I. Huggins, *Afro-American Studies: A Report to the Ford Foundation* (New York: Ford Foundation, 1985).

16. Ibid.

17. "Black Studies Is an Unpopular Major," *The Journal of Blacks in Higher Education* (2003).

18. Painter, "Black Studies, Black Professors, and the Struggles of Perception."

19. Singh, *Black Is a Country: Race and the Unfinished Struggle for Democracy*, 8.

20. Painter, "Black Studies, Black Professors, and the Struggles of Perception."

21. Ibid.

22. Early, "Black Studies: The Good and the Bad."

23. Ibid.

24. Harris, Hine, and McKay, *Black Studies in the United States: Three Essays*.
25. Ibid.
26. Tamar Jacoby, "McGeorge Bundy: How the Establishment's Man Tackled America's Problem with Race," *Alicia Patterson Foundation Magazine* (1991).
27. Kai Bird, *The Color of Truth: McGeorge Bundy and William Bundy, Brothers in Arms: A Biography* (New York: Simon & Schuster, 1998) 394.
28. Bird, 395.
29. Jacoby, "McGeorge Bundy: How the Establishment's Man Tackled America's Problem with Race."
30. Howard Ball, *The Bakke Case: Race, Education, and Affirmative Action* (Lawrence, Kansas: University Press of Kansas, 2000) 2.
31. Ibid.
32. U.S. Supreme Court decision, *The Regents of the University of California v. Bakke*, 438 U.S. 265 (1978).
33. Samantha Hunter, "Panelists Discuss Black Presence in Ivy League," *Columbia News* (April 11, 2004), available online at http://www.columbia.edu/cu/news/04/11/blacks_ivy_league.html.
34. Ibid.
35. Ibid.
36. Harris, Hine, and McKay, *Black Studies in the United States: Three Essays*, 29.
37. Harris, Hine, and McKay, 15.
38. Ibid.

6. EVERYTHING AND NOTHING AT ALL:
RACE, BLACK STUDIES, AND HIGHER EDUCATION TODAY

1. Cecil Brown, "'Dude, Where's My Black Studies Department?' More Africans, Fewer Americans at Cal's African-American Department," *East Bay Express*, Berkeley, December 1, 2004.
2. Felicia Lee, "New Topic in Black Studies Debate: Latinos," *New York Times*, February 1, 2003.
3. Rebecca Stewart, "The 'New' Affirmative Action: A Focus on the Interaction between Affirmative Action and Immigration at Prestigious Universities and Colleges" (unpublished senior thesis, Princeton University, 2005).

4. Sara Rimer and Karen Arenson, "Top Colleges Take More Blacks, but Which Ones?" *New York Times*, June 24, 2004.
5. Ibid.
6. Ibid.
7. Ibid.
8. Ibid.
9. Ibid.
10. Stewart, "The 'New' Affirmative Action."
11. Lee, "New Topic in Black Studies Debate: Latinos."
12. Ibid.
13. Robin Wilson, "Past Their Prime? After 35 Years on Campus, Black Studies Programs Struggle to Survive," *The Chronicle of Higher Education*, April 22, 2005, A 9.
14. Ibid.
15. Robert S. Boynton, "Out of Africa and Back," *New York Times*, March 16, 2002.
16. Rimer and Arenson, "Top Colleges Take More Blacks, but Which Ones?"
17. Wilson, "Past Their Prime? After 35 Years on Campus, Black Studies Programs Struggle to Survive."
18. Ibid.
19. Ibid.
20. Lee, "New Topic in Black Studies Debate: Latinos."
21. Rimer and Arenson, "Top Colleges Take More Blacks, but Which Ones?"
22. Kendra Hamilton, "Challenging the Future of Black Studies," *Black Issues in Higher Education* (March 13, 2003).
23. Ibid.
24. Brown, "'Dude, Where's My Black Studies Department?' More Africans, Fewer Americans at Cal's African-American Department."
25. Rimer and Arenson, "Top Colleges Take More Blacks, but Which Ones?"
26. Ibid.
27. Ibid.
28. Wilson, "Past Their Prime? After 35 Years on Campus, Black Studies Programs Struggle to Survive."
29. Nathan I. Huggins, *Afro American Studies: A Report to the Ford Foundation* (New York: Ford Foundation, 1985).

30. Wilson, "Past Their Prime? After 35 Years on Campus, Black Studies Programs Struggle to Survive."

31. Dwight McBride, "Whither Black Studies?" posted April 19, 2005, in *Chronicle Forums: The Chronicle of Higher Education,* available online at http://chronicle.com/forums/colloquy/archives/2005/04blackstudies.

32. N. Wade, "Scholarly Articles Diverge on Role of Race in Medicine," *New York Times,* March 20, 2003, A30.

33. Ibid.

34. Jenny Strasburg, "Abercrombie & Glitch: Asian Americans Rip Retailer for Stereotypes on T-Shirts," *San Francisco Chronicle,* April 18, 2002, A1.

35. Audrey Davis, "Factors Affecting African American Students' Feelings of Isolation" (unpublished senior thesis, Princeton University, 2002).

SELECTED BIBLIOGRAPHY

Abilla, Walter D. *Source Book in Black Studies*. New York: MSS Information Corp., 1972.

Allen, Robert I. *Dialectics of Black Power*. New York: Weekly Guardian Associates, 1968.

Anderson, Eric, and Alfred A. Moss. *Dangerous Donations: Northern Philanthropy and Southern Black Education, 1902–1930*. Columbia, Missouri: University of Missouri Press, 1999.

Andrews, Lori B. *Black Power, White Blood: The Life and Times of Johnny Spain*. New York: Pantheon Books, 1996.

Armsey, James W. "Interoffice Memorandum: On Black Studies." 1969. Ford Foundation Archives, Office Papers of McGeorge Bundy, Box 1, Folder 5.

Baldwin, James. *The Fire Next Time*. New York: Modern Library, 1995.

Ball, Howard. *The Bakke Case: Race, Education, and Affirmative Action, Landmark Law Cases & American Society*. Lawrence, Kansas: University Press of Kansas, 2000.

Barbour, Floyd B. *The Black Power Revolt: A Collection of Essays*. Boston: Porter Sargent Publishers, 1968.

Barndt, Joseph R. *Why Black Power?* New York: Friendship Press, 1968.

Bartimole, Roldo. "Ralph Locher: A Dose of 1960s History, or, Why Cleveland Mayors are Expendable." 2004. Available online at http://www.lakewoodbuzz.com/RoldoBartimole/RB-08-09-04-Locher.html.

Baruch, Ruth-Marion, and Pirkle Jones. *Black Panthers, 1968*. Los Angeles: Greybull Press, 2002.

Bird, Kai. *The Color of Truth: McGeorge Bundy and William Bundy, Brothers in Arms: A Biography*. New York: Simon & Schuster, 1998.

Black Studies at the Crossroads. Videorecording. Fairfax, Virginia: Cox, Matthews & Associates, 1995.

Blake, Elias, and Henry Cobb, for the Task Force Group for Survey of Afro-American Studies Programs. *Black Studies: Issues in Their Institutional Survival.* Washington, D.C.: U.S. Department of Health, Education, and Welfare, Office of Education, 1976.

Blassingame, John W. *New Perspectives on Black Studies.* Urbana: University of Illinois Press, 1971.

Boynton, Robert S. "The New Intellectuals." *Atlantic Monthly,* March 1995, 53–69.

———. "Out of Africa and Back." *New York Times,* March 16, 2002, 4A, 36.

Bright, Alfred L. *An Interdisciplinary Introduction to Black Studies: History, Sociology, Literature, Art, and Philosophy of Black Civilization.* Dubuque, Iowa: Kendall/Hunt Publishing Co., 1977.

Brown, Cecil. "'Dude, Where's My Black Studies Department?' More Africans, Fewer Americans at Cal's African-American Department." *East Bay Express,* Berkeley, December 1, 2004.

Brown, Scot. *Fighting for Us: Maulana Karenga, the Us Organization, and Black Cultural Nationalism.* New York: New York University Press, 2003.

Bundy, McGeorge. "A Note from the Director." *Ford Foundation Annual Report.* The Ford Foundation, 1967.

Butler, Johnnella E. *Black Studies—Pedagogy and Revolution: A Study of Afro-American Studies and the Liberal Arts Tradition through the Discipline of Afro-American Literature.* Washington, D.C.: University Press of America, 1981.

Clark, Kenneth B. "Letter of Resignation from Board of Directors of Antioch College." In *Black Studies: Myths & Realities,* edited by A. Philip Randolph. New York: A. Philip Randolph Educational Fund, 1969.

Cleaver, Eldridge. *Credo for Rioters and Looters by Eldridge Cleaver, Minister of Information, Black Panther Party.* Alexandria, Virginia: Alexander Street Press, 2003.

———. "Education and the Revolution." *The Black Scholar* 1, no. 1 (1969): 44–52.

Cleaver, Kathleen, and George N. Katsiaficas. *Liberation, Imagination, and the Black Panther Party: A New Look at the Panthers and Their Legacy.* New York: Routledge, 2001.

Columbia Revolt, The. Videorecording. San Francisco: California Newsreel, 1968.

Cross, Theodore L. *The Black Power Imperative: Racial Inequality and the Politics of Nonviolence.* New York: Faulkner, 1984.

Daniel, Philip T. K. *A Report on the Status of Black Studies Programs in Midwestern Colleges and Universities.* De Kalb, Illinois: Northern Illinois University Center for Minority Studies, 1977.

Davies, Lawrence E. "College Head Quits, Criticizing Reagan." *New York Times,* February 23, 1986, 12.

Davis, Audrey. "Factors Affecting African American Students' Feelings of Isolation." Senior thesis, Princeton University, 2002.

Davis, Lenwood G. *A Working Bibliography on Published Materials on Black Studies Programs in the United States.* Monticello, Illinois: Council of Planning Librarians, 1977.

Downs, Donald Alexander. *Cornell '69: Liberalism and the Crisis of the American University.* Ithaca, New York: Cornell University Press, 1999.

Drewry, Henry N. *Black Studies.* Hamilton, Bermuda: Department of Education, 1970.

Early, Gerald. "Black Studies: The Good and the Bad." *New York Times,* April 14, 2002, 4, 34.

Ebony Magazine: The Black Revolution, an Ebony Special Issue. Chicago: Johnson Publishing Co., 1970.

Edwards, Ralph, and Charles Vert Willie. *Black Power/White Power in Public Education.* Westport, Connecticut: Praeger, 1998.

Exum, William H. *Paradoxes of Protest: Black Student Activism in a White University.* Philadelphia: Temple University Press, 1985.

Fager, Charles. *White Reflections on Black Power.* Grand Rapids, Michigan: W. B. Eerdmans Publishing Co., 1967.

Fanon, Frantz. *The Wretched of the Earth.* Translated by Constance Farrington. New York: Grove Press, 1968.

Farber, Jerry. *The Student as Nigger: Essays and Stories.* New York: Pocket Books, 1970.

Fish, John. *Black Power/White Control.* Princeton, New Jersey: Princeton University Press, 1973.

Fisher, Walter. "Memorandum to John Scanlon Re: The Morgan State Negro Studies Syllabus Project." November 8, 1972. Ford Foundation Archives, Office Papers of McGeorge Bundy, Box 1, Folder 5.

————. *Ideas for Black Studies: The Morgan State College Program.* Baltimore: Morgan State College Press, 1971.

Five College Black Studies Executive Committee. *Contributions in Black Studies.* Amherst, Massachusetts: Five College Black Studies Executive Committee.

Ford, Nick Aaron. *Black Studies: Threat-or-Challenge.* Port Washington, New York: Kennikat Press, 1973.

Forman, Seth. *Blacks in the Jewish Mind: A Crisis of Liberalism.* New York: New York University Press, 1998.

Frye, Charles A. *The Impact of Black Studies on the Curricula of Three Universities.* Washington, D.C.: University Press of America, 1976.

————. *Towards a Philosophy of Black Studies.* San Francisco: R & E Research Associates, 1978.

Frye, Hardy T. , Charles C. Irby, and John C. Leggett. *Whither Black Studies?* Stockton, California: Relevant Instructional Materials, 1972.

Gates, Henry Louis Jr. "African American Studies in the 21st Century." *The Black Scholar* (2001): 3–9.

Gayle, Addison. *The Politics of Revolution.* Chicago: Institute of Positive Education, 1972.

Geltman, Max. *The Confrontation: Black Power, Anti-Semitism, and the Myth of Integration.* Englewood Cliffs, New Jersey: Prentice-Hall, 1970.

Geschwender, James A. *The Black Revolt: The Civil Rights Movement, Ghetto Uprisings, and Separatism.* Englewood Cliffs, New Jersey: Prentice-Hall, 1971.

Giles, Raymond H. *Black Studies Programs in Public Schools.* New York: Praeger Publishers, 1974.

Gordon, Jacob U. , and James M. Rosser. *The Black Studies Debate.* Lawrence, Kansas: University of Kansas, 1974.

Goulden, Joseph C. *The Money Givers.* New York: Random House, 1971.

Greaves, William, and Louise Archambault. *Black Power in America: Myth or Reality?* Videorecording. New York: William Greaves Productions, 1988.

Hamilton, Kendra. "Challenging the Future of Black Studies." *Black Issues in Higher Education* (March 13, 1003): 38–39.

Hare, Nathan. "Questions and Answers About Black Studies." In *African American Studies Reader,* edited by Nathaniel Norment Jr.

Durham, North Carolina: North Carolina Academic Press, 2001, 18–22.

Harris, Robert L. *Three Essays: Black Studies in the United States.* New York: Ford Foundation, 1990.

Haskins, James. *Profiles in Black Power.* Garden City, New York: Doubleday, 1972.

Heath, G. Louis. *Off the Pigs! The History and Literature of the Black Panther Party.* Metuchen, New Jersey: Scarecrow Press, 1976.

Hernton, Calvin C. *Coming Together: Black Power, White Hatred, and Sexual Hang-Ups.* New York: Random House, 1971.

Hinshaw, Elton. "Letter to Marion Coolen." 1971. Ford Foundation Archives.

Howe, Harold. "Untitled Interoffice Memorandum to McGeorge Bundy." 1972. Ford Foundation Archives, Office Papers of McGeorge Bundy, Box 1, Folder 6.

Huggins, Nathan I. *Afro-American Studies: A Report to the Ford Foundation.* New York: Ford Foundation, 1985.

Hunter, Samantha. "Panelists Discuss Black Presence in Ivy League." *Columbia News,* April 11, 2004. Available online at http://www.columbia.edu/cu/news/04/11/blacks_ivy_league.html.

Izzard, Charles E. "Letter to John Scanlon." 1969. Ford Foundation Archives, Office Papers of McGeorge Bundy, Box 1, Folder 5.

Jackson, Giovanna R. , and Charles E. Sweet. *Black Nationalism.* Bloomington, Indiana: Indiana University Libraries, 1969.

Jacoby, Tamar. "McGeorge Bundy: How the Establishment's Man Tackled America's Problem with Race." *Alicia Patterson Foundation Magazine* (1991).

James, C. L. R. *Black Power: It's* [sic] *Past, Today, and the Way Ahead.* Lancing, Michigan: Marcus Garvey Institute, 1968.

Jones, Stephen Alan. "The Revolution Will Not Be Televised: Black Studies and the Transformation of American Higher Education, 1967–1972." Unpublished dissertation. Michigan State University, 2003.

Journal of Blacks in Higher Education. 2003. "Black Studies Is an Unpopular Major."

Karenga, Maulana. *Introduction to Black Studies.* Inglewood, California: Kawaida Publications, 1982.

Killian, Lewis M. *The Impossible Revolution, Phase II: Black Power and the American Dream.* 2nd ed. New York: Random House, 1975.

————. *The Impossible Revolution? Black Power and the American Dream*. New York: Random House, 1968.

Lee, Felicia. "New Topic in Black Studies Debate: Latinos." *New York Times*, February 1, 2003, A1.

Lewis, W. Arthur. "Untitled Letter to McGeorge Bundy." 1969. Ford Foundation Archives, Office Papers of McGeorge Bundy, Box 1, Folder 5.

Marable, Manning. *Dispatches from the Ebony Tower: Intellectuals Confront the African American Experience*. New York: Columbia University Press, 2000.

————. *The Road toward Effective Black Power*. Dayton, Ohio: Black Research Associates, 1980.

May 4th Task Force, "The Berkeley Invention Expands." Kent State, 2005. Available online at http://dept.kent.edu/may4/Campus_Unrest/campus_unrest_chapter1d.htm.

McBride, Dwight. "Whither Black Studies?" Posted April 19, 2005, in *Chronicle Forums: The Chronicle of Higher Education*, available online at http://chronicle.com/forums/colloquy/archives/2005/04blackstudies.

————. *Why I Hate Abercrombie & Fitch: Essays on Race and Sexuality*. New York: New York University Press, 2004.

McEvoy, James, and Abraham H. Miller. *Black Power and Student Rebellion*. Belmont, California: Wadsworth Publishing Co., 1969.

Meier, August, John H. Bracey, and Elliott M. Rudwick. *Black Protest in the Sixties*. New York: Markus Wiener Pub., Inc., 1991.

Michel, Claudine, and Jacqueline Bobo. *Black Studies: Current Issues, Enduring Questions*. Dubuque, Iowa: Kendall/Hunt Publishing, 2001.

Morris, Samuel. *The Case and the Course: A Treatise on Black Studies*. London: Committee on Black Studies, 1973.

Muhammad, Akbar. "Letter to Dean Wendell G. Holladay." 1971. Ford Foundation Archives, Office Papers of McGeorge Bundy, Box 1, Folder 5.

Muhammad, David. *The Black Studies Anthology*. Trinidad: Muhammad's Study Group, 1998.

Napper, George. *Blacker Than Thou: the Struggle for Campus Unity*. Grand Rapids, Michigan: Eerdmans, 1973

Newton, James E. *A Curriculum Evaluation of Black Studies in Rela-*

tion to *Student Knowledge of Afro-American History and Culture*. San Francisco: R & E Research Associates, 1976.

New York Times. "Coast College Head Quits Immediately." May 25, 1968, 25.

————. "McGeorge Bundy." August 3, 1966, 4.

————. "Militants' Invasion Paralyzes Campus." November 7, 1968, 50.

Norment, Nathaniel Jr. *The African American Studies Reader*. Durham, North Carolina: Carolina Academic Press, 2001.

O'Connor, Alice. "The Ford Foundation and Philanthropic Activism in the 1960s." In *Philanthropic Foundations: New Scholarship, New Possibilities*, edited by Ellen C. Lagemann. Bloomington, Indiana: Indiana University Press, 1999.

Ogbar, Jeffrey Ogbonna Green. *Black Power: Radical Politics and African American Identity*. Baltimore: Johns Hopkins University Press, 2005.

Ornstein, Allan C. *Urban Education: Student Unrest, Teacher Behaviors, and Black Power*. Columbus, Ohio: Merrill, 1972.

Orrick, William H. *Shut It Down! A College in Crisis: San Francisco State College, October 1968–April 1969. A Report to the National Commission on the Causes and Prevention of Violence*. Washington, D.C.: U.S. Government Printing Office, 1969.

Painter, Nell Irvin. "Black Studies, Black Professors, and the Struggles of Perception." *The Chronicle of Higher Education*, December 15, 2000.

Pantell, Dora F., and Edwin Greenidge. *If Not Now, When? The Many Meanings of Black Power*. New York: Dell, 1969.

Podair, Jerald E. *The Strike That Changed New York: Blacks, Whites, and the Ocean Hill-Brownsville Crisis*. New Haven: Yale University Press, 2002.

"Port Huron Statement." Available online at: lists.village.virginia.edu/ sixties/HTML_docs/Resources/Primary/Manifestos/SDS_Port_ Huron.html.

Rimer, Sara, and Karen Arenson. "Top Colleges Take More Blacks, but Which Ones?" *New York Times*, June 24, 2004, A-1.

Robinson, Armstead L., Craig C. Foster, Donald H. Ogilvie, and Black Student Alliance at Yale. *Black Studies in the University: A Symposium*. New Haven: Yale University Press, 1969.

Rojas, Fabio. "Organizational Decision Making and the Emergence of

Academic Disciplines." Unpublished dissertation, Harvard University, 2002.

Ross, Irwin. "McGeorge Bundy and the New Foundation Style." *Fortune,* April 1968, 107.

Rossiter, Caleb. "Cornell's Student Revolt of 1969: A Rare Case of Democracy on Campus." *The Progressive,* May 5, 1999.

Rustin, Bayard. "Introduction." In *Black Studies: Myths & Realities,* edited by A. Philip Randolph. New York: A. Philip Randolph Educational Fund, 1969, 3–7.

Ryan, Selwyn D., and Taimoon Stewart. *The Black Power Revolution of 1970: A Retrospective.* St. Augustine, Trinidad: University of the West Indies Press, 1995.

San Francisco State College Strike Collection. Special Collections/Archives, J. Paul Leonard Library, San Francisco State University.

Savio, Mario. "Mario Savio's Speech before the Free Speech Movement Sit-In." 1964. Available from The Free Speech Movement Archives Home Page, http://www.fsm-a.org/stacks/mario/mario_speech.html.

Scanlon, James J. "Inter-Office Memorandum to the Files: Seminar on Afro-American Studies Aspen, Colorado." July 19–24, 1971. Ford Foundation Archives, Office Papers of McGeorge Bundy, Box 1, Folder 5.

———. "Interoffice Memorandum to the Files: Afro-American Studies at Morgan State College." March 21, 1969. Ford Foundation Archives, Office Papers of McGeorge Bundy, Box 1, Folder 5.

———. "Where the Rocks Are Likely to Come From." May 21, 1969. Ford Foundation Archives, Office Papers of McGeorge Bundy, Box 1, Folder 5.

Schipper, Martin Paul, Eric Gallagher, and David H. Werning. *Papers of the National Negro Congress.* Frederick, Maryland: University Publications of America, 1988.

Scott, Robert Lee, and Wayne Brockriede. *The Rhetoric of Black Power.* New York: Harper & Row, 1969.

Singh, Nikhil Pal. *Black Is a Country: Race and the Unfinished Struggle for Democracy.* Cambridge, Massachusetts: Harvard University Press, 2004.

Sowell, Thomas. *Affirmative Action around the World: An Empirical Study.* New Haven: Yale University Press, 2004.

Stern, Lawrence, and Richard Harwood. "Ford Foundation: Its Works Spark Backlash." *Washington Post,* November 2, 1969.

Stewart, Rebecca. "The 'New' Affirmative Action: A Focus on the Interaction between Affirmative Action and Immigration at Prestigious Universities and Colleges." Unpublished senior thesis, Princeton University, 2005.

Stokes, Carl B. *Promises of Power: A Political Autobiography*. New York: Random House, 1971.

Strasburg, Jenny. "Abercrombie & Glitch: Asian Americans Rip Retailer for Stereotypes on T-Shirts." *San Francisco Chronicle*, April 18, 2002, A1.

Summerskill, John. *President Seven*. New York: World Publishing Co., 1971.

Thibodeaux, Mary Roger. *A Black Nun Looks at Black Power*. New York: Sheed & Ward, 1972.

Thomas, Gail E., ed. *Black Students in Higher Education: Conditions and Experiences in the 1970s*. Westport, Connecticut: Greenwood Press, 1981.

Turner, Wallace. "Classes Resume after Protest at College on Coast." *New York Times*, December 3, 1968, 29.

———. "Police Repel Students at College in San Francisco." *New York Times*, December 4, 1968, 26.

Vivian, C. T. *Black Power and the American Myth*. Philadelphia: Fortress Press, 1970.

Voices in Black Studies. Bloomington, Indiana: National Council for Black Studies, Indiana University.

Wagstaff, Thomas. *Black Power: The Radical Response to White America*. Beverly Hills, California: Glencoe Press, 1969.

Wilcox, Preston, ed. *Black Power Conference Reports*. New York: AFRAM Associates, 1970.

Wilcox, Preston. *A Think Piece: The Multiple Forms of Black Studies Programs*. Harlem, New York: National Association for African American Education, 1970.

Wilkins, Roger. "Inter-Office Memorandum from Roger Wilkins to McGeorge Bundy Re: Afro-American Studies." May 22, 1969. Ford Foundation Archives, Office Papers of McGeorge Bundy, Box 1, Folder 5.

Wilkins, Roy. "The Case against Separatism: 'Black Jim Crow.'" In *Black Studies: Myths & Realities*, edited by A. Philip Randolph. New York: A. Philip Randolph Educational Fund, 1969, 33–39.

Williams, Yohuru. *Black Politics/White Power: Civil Rights, Black*

Power, and the Black Panthers in New Haven. St. James, New York: Brandywine Press, 2000.

Williamson, Joy Ann. *Black Power on Campus: The University of Illinois, 1965–75.* Urbana: University of Illinois Press, 2003.

Wilson, Robin. "Past Their Prime? After 35 Years on Campus, Black Studies Programs Struggle to Survive." *The Chronicle of Higher Education,* April 22, 2005, A9.

Woodard, Komozi, and Randolph Boehm. *The Black Power Movement.* Bethesda, Maryland: University Publications of America, 2000.

Wright, Nathan, Jr. *Black Power and Urban Unrest.* New York: Hawthorn Books, Inc., 1969.

Wright, Sylvia Hart. *Black Youth, Black Studies, and Urban Education: A Study of Use Patterns in Two Innovative New York Libraries.* New York: City University of New York, 1975.

INDEX

academic legitimacy of African
American Studies, 115–16,
123–24, 125, 126, 127–31,
144
academic vs. vocational education for Blacks, 103, 104–5
admissions. *See* recruitment of
minority students; quotas,
admission
affirmative action: and Black
faculty developments, 125–
26, 133–34, 135–36; and
Black Studies as recruitment
tool, 126–31, 133, 135–36,
142; and immigrants vs.
native-born Black Ameri-
cans, 158, 159; reverse discrimination challenge, 27,
145–51. *See also* Supreme
Court
African American Studies: contemporary profile, 123–26,
135–46; current challenges
to, 159; discipline vs. field
identity for, 150–51; enrollment losses, 129–30; future
prospects, 165–77; in post–
civil rights era, 131–34;
re-segregation and affirmative action, 126–31; and

shifting Black demographics,
160–62, 165; and shift to
African Diaspora studies,
151–53; scholastic respectability of, 115–16, 123–24,
125, 126, 127–31, 144. *See
also* Black Studies
African American vs. Black
identity, 123–25, 127, 142–
43, 152, 155–65, 167–68
African Diaspora studies move-
ment, 151–53, 161, 163–64
African immigrants, 152,
155–65
Afro-American studies. *See*
Black Studies
Afrology, 73
Ali, Muhammad, 46
Allen, Robert, 87
anti-Semitism, Black, 91
Arenson, Karen, 157–58
armed occupations by students,
56–59
Armey, Dick, 11
Armsey, James, 99–100
Asian immigrants/Asian Ameri-
cans, 172–73
Atkins, Keletso E. , 162
Atlantic Monthly, 123–24, 146
autonomy. *See* Black Studies

Printed in the United States
By Bookmasters